I AM WHO I AM!

The "closed book" of

MARK DUNKIN
Kevin Ward

Independent Publishing Network

I AM WHO I AM! The "closed book" of

Written by Mark Dunkin

CONTENTS

INTRODUCTION

My life has been eventful with many trials and tribulations. I live with a positive outlook as I am the only one who can make my life happy, make me succeed, and even though at times I haven't felt this way. I am proud of all I have achieved and the man I have become.

This has been written with me being as honest and open as I can be, it is from my own personal perspective and view.

It has not been written to make anyone else feel they had a negative impact on my life, because regardless of what part they have played, I am extremely grateful to everyone who has known me and contributed to making me who I am today.

I would also like to remind everyone that every situation does have two sides, and even though I have done my best to writc from my own recollection, other people will have their own beliefs, thoughts and memories which may differ from my own.

I've split this book into chapters titled by major events of my life which happen to be relationships, I knew happiness was in my hands.

I have managed throughout my life by simply turning the page and starting a new chapter, which even though I didn't realise at the time has made this book easier to structure. This book ends when I got married to Anne-Marie in October 2023, when I was 45 years young.

DON'T GIVE UP

When things go wrong as
they sometimes will,
When the road you're trudging
Seems all uphill,
When funds are low
and debts are high,
And you want to smile
but you have to sigh,
When care is pressing
you down a bit,
Rest, if you must,
But don't you quit

Author unknown

I AM WHO I AM!

CHAPTER 1

Childhood

This adventure started on a road in a suburb of Norwich called Hellesdon. There were houses on one side and trees a couple of metres back from the kerb on the other. My parents and older sister Lynn-Ann moved into the property shortly after she was born, the house was a new build, and they were the first family to move into these three bed properties.

I was born back in the days before mobile phones, fortunately there was a red phone box just up the road on a small green. Upon contacting the midwife my dad found that they were further down the road, so he ran to get assistance. I came into this world at 07:20 in the morning after a short labour and it has been said that my mum then sat in bed recovering, eating fresh hot cross buns and I guess a black coffee.

As one can expect, I remember little from my early years, made more difficult with events that happened later in life which you will find out more about later in this adventure, but I will be writing about as much as I remember during this journey.

Not long after my second birthday, for reasons unknown to myself my mum moved out. It was decided both my sister and I would remain in the family home with my dad, keeping regular contact so we had stability and a roof over our heads.

In time, both my parents recoupled and got married.

I recall my mum living in a flat above my grandparents' shop near Anglia Square.

My brother Andy was born a couple of years later. I remember my mum, her husband and my brother living above a pub they ran in the centre of Norwich. I vaguely remember going down and raiding the freezer for a Jubbly (strangely shaped ice pop things).

I attended a playgroup in Hellesdon when my sister started school and we had a child minder who lived close by. Life for my mum was not great in her marriage with her husband, so that relationship dissolved and unfortunately for Andy his dad did not keep in contact. Both Lynn-Ann and I were still living with my dad. On the Sunday we used to go along to St Catherine's church where I attended the Sunday school out in the back room. After church we often used to walk to the toy shop to get sweets. A chain stopped you going past the sweets and papers due to the Sunday trading laws.

In my earlier years we spent many summer holidays with my mum at a caravan park in my grandparents' static caravan, firstly in Hopton and later in Hemsby.

My mum moved to a property that was connected to a butcher's shop in Mile Cross. Many vague memories of this time; being allowed to watch the butcher make sausages;

creeping out early to collect up the local Co-op stamp books that had escaped from the local shop; going to the post office to get a mixed bag of penny sweets/chews. The property had the kitchen and lounge downstairs, a wooden staircase leading upstairs to a large room/landing where my mum slept, with two bedrooms off that (my brother and I shared one while my sister had the other), along with another door for the bathroom. I remember being told that one night I came out of my room, sleepwalking. My mum asked where I was going, and I answered I was going to play on the slide, pointing to the stairs. For obvious reasons I was quickly ushered back to bed.

I vaguely remember my mum seeing a chap who lived out near Barford, near Norwich. If my memory serves me correctly, he had two sons and there was a road running past the end of his back garden as well as in front, with fields on the other side.

When of school age I attended the local school, where I was a cheeky little Chappy. I recall making a clay object to symbolise Halley's comet (which will next be visible from earth in August 2061). I have vague memories of my stepmum taking me to school in the mornings and playing/queuing in the playground, the times we had P.E. which involved stripping down to pants/vest and walking through the corridors to the hall with a wooden floor, which also doubled as the canteen at lunchtime. Also, one year on my birthday I was collected by my mum in a yellow Mercedes estate 7-seater (fold-down seats in the boot which faced the rear) so we could be taken to McDonalds with friends for my birthday party.

Many times during my younger years, I recall visiting my grandparents in Holland-on-Sea, Essex. I have many happy memories here, mostly during school holidays. My grandad used to keep canaries among other small birds in his shed/ aviary in the garden; being taken down to the beach in the summer and on one occasion getting severely sunburnt with big blisters on my shoulders (having to have a bath to remove my t-shirt); going along to whist drives (a card game) at the local club where my grandparents proudly introduced us to friends and we would help with the raffle; the time I went with grandad to collect promotional packs of playing cards from a Shell garage with tokens collected at the whist drives (I still have a pack in my memory box); the time I was allowed to hold the lead and walk my uncle's dog but unfortunately it got hurt and had to go to the vet; how we all used to sit round an oak table at dinner times; my nanny making the best ever coffee cakes; and at Easter how my grandad would hide eggs of different sizes for us to find either in the front room or in the garden; the year of bad snow we got stuck on the way back to Norwich and were towed by a tractor to The Magpie PH on the A140 to sit out the snow (I slept under or near the pool table). I recall the time we were celebrating my dad's birthday around the oak dining table, the phone rang and it was my uncle to inform us that my cousin had just been born, and whenever visiting we always played card games, a favourite at Christmas time was Newmarket.

After a while, I remember my mum moving in with her partner, who lived in a 3-bedroom bungalow in a cul-de-sac in Old Catton. He owned a maroon Triumph TR6 two-seater and on the day of their wedding he reversed into a bollard at the end of the drive. Later he had a beige Rover SD1 so we could all go out as a family. My mum moved with her husband to a 4-bedroom new build with a double garage which was next to a primary school. The new road also ran next to a park. When they lived here, I remember many minor things I got up to, exploring the building site and going knee deep in sandy puddles, climbing over the fence into the school to retrieve our football, the time I made a go-kart and the wheel came off, which in turn trapped my finger between the frame and ground resulting in me losing a nail and needing medical attention. I also remember, it was while living here that I had the good old blue Boxer bike, and if my memory serves me right my brother had the purple Tomahawk.

I also recall my grandparents moving to The Lodge in Lower Hellesdon, if my memory serves me correctly it had thirty-six doors, seven bedrooms and a swimming pool in the garden. My earliest memory of the house is shortly after they moved in a friend came round and we ran into the empty swimming pool and tried to reach the top of the deep end, we thought it was just a pile of leaves but underneath was rainwater. I have countless memories from here and of my grandparents. We spent most Saturdays here with my mum, as all my cousins did. Ceefax was always on the television for the football scores.

One year I remember one of my uncles taking me to Kent for an airshow with his girlfriend (future wife) and her daughter (my future cousin). I don't really remember the air-show but I do recall letting tissues go out the window as we drove through the Dartford Tunnel.

I recall going on holiday with my dad and stepmum to Majorca. We went with a colleague from dad's work and his wife. The standout memory from this holiday was swimming out to a small rock island. While climbing out dad slipped and sliced his toe. A day or two later, back at the apartment someone came out of the bathroom asking why the sugar was in there. Dad had been bathing his foot in sugar water instead of salt water.

For reasons I am unsure of, I then remember my mum separating and moving to another house in Old Catton. Ian Culverhouse (Norwich City player) lived in a property opposite. The day my mum moved, my stepdad reversed the Rover into a concrete bollard at the end of the shared drive. While we were living here, there was one time I was doing my bit to help by cutting the grass in the garden with a Flymo. Being young, I was not aware that you were not supposed to run over the lead, and me being me, I picked both ends up and tried to put them back together. This blew the fuse for the whole house.

My middle school adjoined my first school. I played for several of the sports teams. One incident I recall is when we played football against St Edmund's in Taverham. We lost. On the minibus trip home, we were larking around and I got reported for pulling a moony out the back window. And this was the reason I was kicked off the team. I also attended the local cubs at the troop down the track beside the school. What was special about this troop is that my mum's dad helped build the hut many years before. There is a photo somewhere of when it was first built. Cubs taught me the basics for life as well as the camaraderie of friendship, I also played for the cubs' football team, as well as the local team, which was coached by Ian Culverhouse. It was at some point during these years that I started cycle speedway for Norwich Stars.

Around this time, my mum started dating her future fourth husband, who ran a business repairing and selling televisions. His place of work was in my grandparents' unit, and he often did work for them, delivering or helping when deliveries arrived.

It was during the later years of middle school for me when Lynn-Ann went to live with my mum (my parents still kept to alternate weekends and half school holidays for us), but during the holidays I used to go into my grandparents' business (aerial manufacture and electronic wholesale), where I assisted in the office by sorting paperwork into filing cabinets, or in the manufacturing department putting nuts on U-bolts and the screws in the terminals in preparation for the people making the aerials. Around this time, the business moved to a bigger unit further down the close, where storage shelves and stud walls were built. I was helping my uncle in supporting some eight-by-four sheets which slipped and trapped me underneath. My uncle immediately shouted for help, but before it arrived he had picked up one end so I could crawl out. This uncle also used to fix up cars as he had done an apprenticeship as a mechanic with Porsche when he first left school before he came to work for the business. I often used to help him work on the vehicles or earn some pocket money by T-cutting or polishing them for him.

Around this time, my stepmum was contacted by her biological son, who she had given up for adoption at birth due to personal circumstances; he came to live with us for a brief time. He found work as a sales assistant at River Island. However, for reasons unknown to me at the time, he soon left. I have since found out that he was a liar and a thief, which affected my stepmum mentally. I guess, with other reminders from her past this caused her to have a mental breakdown, which resulted in her getting admitted/sectioned into David Rice Hospital. It was near to our house, so I used to cycle up and visit after school regularly. When my stepmum left the hospital, she could not face coming back to the house, so she rented a room from a friend in the city before moving to a ground floor flat in Lakenham.

I remember attending Villa Park with my grandad and uncles to watch Norwich City play Everton in the FA Cup semi-final and hearing of the event at Hillsborough as it unfolded on the handheld radio one of them was carrying so we could keep track of the other score.

I attended various groups/clubs; scouts at a troop in Drayton, where I gained many experiences which have come in helpful during my life (camping, cooking, knots, discipline). Youth club was at the local Methodist church (darts, pool, table tennis, cards, amongst other activities organised by the leaders).

I remember for my twelfth birthday staying at my uncle's the night prior and going to the Radio1 roadshow at Alton Towers with staff from the aerial department at the family business. I believe this was also the year I went with my uncle to Snetterton racetrack for a 24hr event and Brands Hatch racetrack for a weekend racing event.

I attended Hellesdon High School with many of my class friends from middle school, also gaining others from other schools in the area, and even though I kept myself busy with groups/clubs I started mixing with the wrong crowd after school while my dad was still at work and sometimes at weekends. Doing things I am not proud of, but they happened so have been dealt with and I must live with the memories.

In the December of 1991, my mum and stepdad moved into a property in Thorpe Marriott. After Christmas, I had been into town with friends and we had been getting up to mischief, and I recall being in the arcade at the Christmas fair. This was situated on Castle Meadow in the centre of Norwich. That evening was their housewarming party, so I needed to be home on time. I got the bus and at my stop on Fakenham Road, I got off and ran behind the bus, straight into the path of a white Ford Escort estate. A fair bit of what follows is from things I have been told or learned from various sources due to the injuries I received. The Escort gained a smashed headlight, dented bonnet, smashed windscreen and bent A pillar. The only information I had with me about who I was or where I lived were the estate agent's property information sheet. I have been told that while waiting for the ambulance to arrive the only understandable faint noise to come from my mouth was "bulance". Seconds later, others heard the sirens as the ambulance approached. The police went to my mum's address to find only Lynn-Ann at home as everyone else was out doing the last bit of shopping for the party. I have been told Lynn-Ann was asked "When will your parents be home?", "Have you got a brother?" and "Is he into Airfix models?". When my mum returned, she was informed I had been involved in an R.T.A, in a serious condition and had been taken to the N&N Hospital. I assume my mum then contacted my dad before making her way to the hospital where she met up with my dad. I recall being told that when they arrived I was already being seen to. They sat my parents down and told them to prepare themselves as I was in a critical state, hooked up to a life support machine, with a fractured skull, right ankle and left little finger, that I only had a 10% chance of surviving and if I did it was likely I would be stuck in a wheelchair. I like to think the damage caused to the Escort was caused by me trying to jump the car as it came towards me: My right ankle broke the light, the bonnet got dented by me landing on it (which fractured my little finger) at the same time as my head hitting the A-pillar, which smashed the screen and caused my fractured skull.

CHAPTER 2

Teenage years

The following days were very touch and go, a blood clot formed on my brain and I was living on the life support machine while in an induced coma. Obviously, I have little memory of this time as the brain is an amazing organ which blocks out traumatic times. It also makes writing this difficult as there are periods of time where I cannot put events into chronological order: I just have vague memories. I only have a few vivid memories from my time in hospital:

- Very few people have been made aware of this as I feel I may get judged, but I recall swimming/floating on my own down a dark corridor/tunnel with a figure stood at the end. I never made it to the figure, I guess if I had I would not be here today and that this is the point when I came out of the coma.
- I recall being pushed along a corridor through the basement in a wheelchair with my ankle in plaster.

- This must have been a couple of months afterwards, but I remember sitting in a wheelchair with my mum and dad nearby waiting for a meeting with the Neurology specialist, Mr Brain.
- I remember attending physiotherapy at the hospital with Penny - who knows why I remember her name! She aided my physical strength building and coordination, I also attended The Clare School which was a specialist place I attended for occupational therapy to aid my neurological recovery.

Because of my injuries, I was not allowed to play sports for a good six months after being discharged from hospital, which meant my love of most sports faded but my interest in outdoor activities grew. When my personal belongings were returned there were earphones, cigarettes, matches and a couple of 14 ml Revell paint pots which I can only assume I acquired wrongfully.

The positive of my RTA is that this got my parents communicating again and putting their past behind them.

Even though I couldn't place this in order chronologically, I attended the semi-final when Norwich City played Southampton at Hillsborough. My memory is very vague, but I believe I won the minibus sweepstake and we stopped at a pub en route home near Mildenhall.

I recall the occasion when I was first allowed to go into the city with friends, and I was silly enough to go with friends who had been a bad influence previously. We were in HMV, which was in the same building as Topshop, and I stole a single (before the days of CD's). Upon leaving the shop I was followed by the store detective and apprehended. He took me back into the store, to an office in the back to question me and wait till the time I was meeting my dad so he could talk with him (in those days mobile phones were a rare object). When we met with my dad and information was passed on, I was in big trouble. Christmas presents were banned that year and I had to miss birthday presents the following year. I was not grounded but had a 18:00 curfew, so I had the embarrassment of telling friends I had to be home.

My interests started changing. I had canoe lessons down near Dolphin bridge on the river Wensum where I gained a few certificates, I got more involved at the Methodist church, where I became a Christian and went along to services on a Sunday evening and was regularly away any chance I could, hiking or camping with scouts in the Peak District or Yorkshire.

I recall going to watch Norwich City play Bayern Munich at home in the UEFA cup. We lost, which was a disappointment. What was more depressing was when I got home I found the Police and forensic teams there, as my dad had got home to find we had been broken into. The burglars had gained access via the conservatory and prising open the rear window. It was mainly electrical items taken from downstairs and the bedrooms.

Even though my upbringing was structured to a degree (alternate weekends and holidays split between parents) and with both my parents in decent jobs, personally I did not always find it happy and plain sailing. When I needed time out during my teens I used to visit the Drayton woods nearby. I used to sit at the edge which looked out over the fields where I could chill, think about life, cry if need be, and chat things through with my imaginary friend whilst listening to the birds sing, hearing the occasional car or motorcycle travelling down an adjacent road and at rare times watch a plane coming in or taking off from the nearby airport. Even though Christmases and birthdays were always enjoyable (getting to celebrate twice) it sometimes didn't seem fair. One year I recall getting a Sony Discman with some CD's and even though my parents always picked me up/dropped me off, on this occasion I decided to walk the 5K to my mum's so I could clear my head. I was walking down the Fakenham Rd with it raining gently, the discman headphones over my ears listening to Bon Jovi and "Keep the Faith" began to play, and so right it was to me.

The Christmas when I was fourteen, I decided to do a sponsored 24hr fast to raise money for the local housing shelter. I also decided I would go along to St Andrew's Hall to help any way I could in feeding the homeless/lonely. The fast was to start at midday on Christmas Day through to midday Boxing Day. By doing it this way I would be asleep less time and the challenge would be harder. I was at my mum's that year and Lynn-Ann kindly offered to drive me into the city. The roads were quiet as most people were at home with families. I entered the hall to be cheerfully invited in, several tables and chairs were being set out while I spoke to the organiser explaining why I wanted to help and about my fast. I was put to work straight away, helping with the setup and occasionally I would see people enter with boxes of gifts or presents they were donating. I popped outside for a cigarette shortly before the doors opened, a queue was already forming and the organiser spotted that I was smoking roll-ups so he offered me a change of role which I gladly accepted. I was now chief roll-up maker as they had received donations of several pouches of rolling tobacco and papers. I got straight to work so they could be handed out when people were arriving. Someone came over shortly before midday and handed me a bunch of bananas to eat as they had heard of my fast. I stopped rolling and managed to eat five before it got to mid-day, I have no idea how many roll-ups were made but I know people left with their pockets filled. After I had been here, I went to The Lodge in Hellesdon where we always spent Christmas Eve or New Year's Eve (depending on when I was with mum), the whole extended family would meet there to celebrate together.

On New Year's Day this year I was baptised at Meadow Way Chapel in Hellesdon wearing a black Jack Daniels t-shirt and black combat trousers.

I recall going on a day trip with my dad over to Belgium via ferry from Felixstowe, I nearly brought a new mountain bike but decided against it. This is also where I first had mayonnaise with chips which was a total game changer for me and instigated my love of mayonnaise rather than ketchup.

A month before my sixteenth birthday, I went to live with my mum and joined Army cadets as I had decided I was going to apply to join the Army just after my birthday. I completed my CBT and bought myself a red Vespa (reg. H180 TVG). I thought I was the bee's knees with my black leather jacket (present off my dad), black Shoei helmet (present from my stepmum), army boots and black cargo trousers (bought from the surplus store). I bought a chrome backrest for it and while fitting/making slight adjustments I slipped and put the chisel into my left hand. It was when living with my mum I started attending church at Drayton Hall.

This same year my stepmum was diagnosed with breast cancer and I remember visiting the hospital just after her operation to find her outside puffing away only a few hours after surgery. I thought it was great having the freedom to go where I wanted when I wanted within reason.

Around this time, I used to cut my uncle's grass for extra money, and his neighbour Herbie Hide (WBB Heavyweight champion) asked if I would cut his for £10 (double what I usually charged my uncle). I remember this as it was over knee height before I started, and I didn't quite finish it. A week or so later I got a message from my auntie saying he wished to see me. I went straight round, expecting him to ask when I would be returning to finish, but instead he said he didn't have any change and handed me a £20 note.

When it came to taking my GCSEs I wasn't overly interested, revision was minimal as I had spent my school years learning and in my eyes that had been enough. Back when I did my exams, everyone sat in the same hall at the start of the test, and when it came time the lower groups would get up and leave the room. My expected grades were C's and D's, me being me though, I got up and out as soon as I could.

In Army cadets I was doing my Gold Duke of Edinburgh award. On our last expedition we were on the Pen-y-fan in Wales, we had just used our survival bags as sledges to descend from the peak and we came across a hiker who had fallen and seriously injured his knee, so between us we orchestrated a rescue to the bottom to meet the ambulance crew. I recall very few details but I do remember a couple of weeks later there was a small article in our local paper thanking us.

I was not accepted into the Army that year but was told to reapply the following year. So, the Monday after my last GCSE exam, (4th July to be exact), I started fulltime at my family business, working as an office junior. When my results came out, 1 C, 4 D's, 3 E's and 1 F, I was told I had to return to sixth form as my grades were not up to scratch. I returned to sixth form to do a GNVQ in Business Studies where I progressed well, but within a couple of months I decided it was not for me as my heart was still set on joining the Army. So I left the sixth form and went to the Careers Office to re-apply. The following week I started at an engineering college on the airport industrial estate where I gained two NVQ's within five months, one in electrical engineering and one in machine engineering.

Two weeks after my seventeenth birthday I went for my full motorcycle test, which I passed, but I was not allowed to use my savings to buy a motorcycle, so I had some driving lessons and passed my driving test the following month. I also found out I had been accepted for the Army and would be joining in the August. The next couple of months I spent working for an agency, going through my belongings, and selling all I could before I started my new life.

The night before I travelled to Bassingbourn Barracks, a family gathering and BBQ was organised at my mum's so family could say goodbye. The following morning, my mum and stepdad took me to the train station to say their final farewells. I arrived at Royston station where a coach was waiting to take us to the barracks. There were several recruits, they were easily spotted as they had large bags or suitcases and some were carrying an ironing board to save buying one in the NAAFI shop. We were on parade before entering the billet when recruit Teale (professional footballer Shaun Teale's son) arrived late, coming straight from the airport after a family holiday. He had a kit inspection in front of us all and was mocked for having several condoms in a pocket on his rucksack. Corporal Dare was my section Corporal and Sergeant Walker oversaw the section. A couple of weeks into basic training, my knee started giving me grief, a couple more weeks passed and I was trying to ignore the discomfort, but I was having to cause pain elsewhere to deal with the pain. It was on a long march/run that I was caught hitting myself which resulted in me being withdrawn from training. I recall the first camp out where we made our shelters but I was not allowed to take part in the activity so was left looking after the section's weapons. A week later I was moved to Gallipoli, the rehab section, while I received treatment. After four weeks in Gallipoli I had a meeting with the section commander who informed me it didn't look as though I'd get back into training for another eight weeks, which would have meant six months on camp before I'd pass out, so I took the decision to apply for free discharge as I was still seventeen and I thought it wouldn't be held on record if I reapplied at a later date. It was during my time in Gallipoli that we spent all night manning the disused airfield as a Battalion was stopping over en route back from Germany to refuel and take in food. Bassingbourn Barracks has been used for filming some sections of the films Full Metal Jacket and Memphis Belle.

Upon leaving the Army in late October, I went straight to

the beer festival to help as I had done for the previous years as my dad helped organise it. I also found my dad had moved from my birth home two weeks earlier and my mum was moving the following day. I am sure they were both trying to escape me. I moved back to my mum's while I organised somewhere else to live, I registered with a doctor in Drayton due to my injuries and was given a sick note while I received treatment on my knees. This was where I found out that my injuries were scar tissue on the underside of both kneecaps as well as ligament/muscle strains. It was at this time I subconsciously decided sports would no longer play a part in my life and I stopped going to church.

I got a job testing electrical equipment before and after repairs, but I found this work tedious, so after talking to my stepdad he agreed he would give me work until I found further employment. I soon found some work as a spray shop assistant/driver, which was cut short as I scraped their van. A couple of weeks later I started at Dunston Hall as a waiter in the carvery. It was during this time I moved into a caravan at the end of my dad's garden on a country lane between Hethersett and Wymondham. Even though I enjoyed the work as I was kept busy, hospitality did not suit the lifestyle I wanted so I took a temporary position as a kitchen porter in an office block where I worked Monday – Friday. When this position ended, I helped in the family business a couple of times before they took me on fulltime in the sales department.

It was during this time that Lynn-Ann got married, and this is where I met Tanya, who was the sister of a girl my mum was fostering. She also lived in foster care but elsewhere. A few months later, when the colder weather came, I was fortunate enough to be offered a bedsit in Bowthorpe, which was closer to work.

It was around this time that I got my first mobile phone and I started working for my family business in the sales department. Most Saturdays, I would travel to Mansfield with a full van and quite often a trailer to deliver aerials to two customers, and on occasion stop at a supplier's to collect stock so I wasn't travelling back empty. It was during one of these trips I got points on my driving licence for the first time, as I was caught speeding down Leadenham hill on the A17. My uncle was shocked due to the van's top speed, but I enjoyed coasting down in neutral, just wasn't expecting a policeman to catch me with a speed gun across a field.

CHAPTER 3

Tanya

I had been living in Bowthorpe for a short time when my uncle offered me a small one bed flat above Wrights near the airport in Hellesdon. Things between Tanya and myself were going well when she sprung on me that life at her foster home was not great and if I did not let her move in she was going to live on the streets. I organised for her to move in with me. It was while living there that Channel 5 was first aired, and I clearly remember Lady Diana dying as it was while we were waiting to leave to visit my nanny in Holland-on-Sea for her birthday. The relationship with Tanya wasn't perfect, we were both young after all, but I recall two visits I had to make to the hospital, one for a cut on my left hand that required stitches after a disagreement, and another which resulted in me fracturing my right hand after I punched a wall in frustration (I told people the spanner slipped off a nut when I was working on my car). After a while we were offered a bigger flat above a television shop in Hellesdon. We moved in, and as money was short with only me working, it was common that we spent Sundays visiting car boot sales, either buying or selling. There was one occasion when a friend stayed with us as he had no-where else to stay. It was not for long though as I often came home to find him drunk. On the last occasion I challenged him, only to be attacked with a metal bed leg which ended in me having to attend A&E with a severe cut on my head that required stitches. Not long after this, things between Tanya and myself got too much and she decided to go and stay at her sister's while she looked for somewhere different to live. Finances meant that I also looked for somewhere else to live and I ended up moving in with a friend I worked with in Mile Cross who owned a house on the old RSPCA site.

Not long after I moved in, Tanya moved into support and lodgings not too far away and we started seeing each other more often again. Not living together reduced the stresses between us. A brief time later we found out Tanya was pregnant, so we applied for a council house while still living separately. A month passed, and when I popped to see Tanya there was an issue with her support worker, so I had to call the emergency services. This resulted in the police attending, who then contacted a crisis team, and the carer was sectioned under the Mental Health Act, which meant Tanya was moved to a different support and lodgings facility.

Four months before Tanya's due date, we were offered a first floor, two-bedroom council flat in Heartsease. It wasn't exactly what we wanted, but the area was nice, and the next offer may have been in an area where we didn't wish to live, so we accepted with the idea of me moving straight in to decorate and set the home up in preparation so they could both move in when our child was born. I moved in with no furniture, I had a mattress on the floor to sleep on and only a few basic things so I could function and look after myself at the flat. By the time the due date came, the flat was decorated and furnished, with items I had scrounged or picked up cheap from car boot sales or charity shops. The second room was set up in gender neutral colours as our baby's sex was unknown. This is when Tanya officially moved in, although she had stayed over a few times previously. Ten days later I was woken by Tanya who was having stomach pains. I called the maternity suite who told me to take her in. I had recced the quickest route, having driven different routes at various times of the day in preparation. Tanya's water broke en route to the hospital. We arrived at the hospital at six in the morning and I was lucky enough to be able to park near the entrance doors. The lifts were just a short distance down the corridor. Upon arrival we were put in a room that had a birthing pool. After an hour or so we were informed there was still plenty of time as nothing had progressed, so I was sent home to collect some bits that Tanya forgot to pack. After collecting the required items, on my way back to the hospital I popped into work to inform them (a lot of them were my extended family) about the reason for my absence. We sat at the hospital all day with regular checks and inspections but not a lot was changing. Tanya even had a dip in the pool in case it helped but she decided it was not for her. Georgina eventually entered the world at 01:52 in the morning of the day after our arrival at the hospital. Both mother and daughter were fit and healthy. I had held it together the whole time until I popped out of the room to update my parents, then the emotions hit me, and I sobbed like a baby but pulled myself together before re-entering the room.

It was around this time I realised Tanya had major issues with Jealousy. I knew there had always been little episodes but it got to the stage where I was not even watching the television when it was on so I didn't get accused of fancying one of the actresses.

After Georgina's birth we didn't get out too much due to money and me working whenever I could. If we did it was commonly, for a drive and occasionally if money permitted we would have a McDonalds. I say we, but Tanya would have a meal and I'd share the drink while I would have a cheeseburger; once Georgina started eating solids it would be a meal for Tanya and a cheeseburger happy meal for Georgina so she could have fries and Tubbie toast (the bread bun) I would get the drink and burger on its own. It was while going for drives we would often try and follow hot air balloons; I knew one of the pilots from work as we supplied his shop. As he had seen me regularly, he asked if we wanted to join his crew, which we did and he took us to a balloon meet where I got to tether in G-ORAC which was the RAC van. The following year he had hot air balloon G-LAMP built, which was in the shape of a standard light bulb.

I was still working for the family business, where I was now in charge of the lighting (lamps) department, with my own small unit for surplus stock which would not fit on the shelves in the main warehouse, working all hours possible to survive financially. During a disagreement at home with Tanya, which was over money, it came about that she would leave with Georgina and I would not see her again. So I did the silly thing and said we would get married. We agreed the day between our birthdays which would have been a Friday just over six weeks away. My family couldn't close the business on a Friday, so we agreed to get married on the Saturday (my 22nd birthday), everyone came together and made it happen. It was only going to be a simple day, but family would be attending.

On the morning of the wedding, I was up at my normal time and left the house, dropping my suit at a neighbour's where I would be getting ready. Then I went to get my hair cut by my regular barber on the estate. On my return to the neighbour's house I had a basic cooked breakfast ready for me which I ate before getting ready. My brother Andy was my best man and arrived with a bottle of Jack Daniels which we opened. Once dressed and ready, we sat drinking, waiting for my uncle who was our lift, but by the time he arrived the bottle was empty. On the way to the family business where we were meeting some other family members, I recall a replica Batmobile passing us as we drove over St Crispin's flyover, as there was a Comic Con event on in the city, and the current No.1 "Uptown girl" by Westlife playing on the radio. At the registry office after the ceremony, I remember being in the gardens at the rear when an old vehicle pulled in. I turned to Andy, jokingly saying "I feel sorry for whoever has got that", only to be ushered over to the car by my stepdad as he had organised it for us. We then headed to the airport hotel for our wedding breakfast with my dad's side of the family and Tanya's family. On arrival, I have been caught on camera telling dad to keep an eye on me and not to let me drink any more alcohol. After the meal we were taken to my uncle and auntie's in Horsford which is where our evening reception was being held as our wedding gift. I guess the evening went well: I remember very little of it due to my alcohol intake in the morning, but I do recall one of my uncles turning up with a tray of shots while we were congregated in the garage and a short speech by another uncle telling everyone about the time I accompanied him to a job in Dereham a few years earlier and where I was told that Fred the fish, who lived in the lake, would surface if I called him. So obviously me being me, I stood on the bank of the lake calling Fred. I cannot recall making it into bed that night.

Life was now settling a bit and I was feeling more comfortable with life, so I applied to the council for "the right to buy" the flat, and even though funds were short I started a personal pension. In the August I spoke with the family business as money was so tight and we were seriously struggling, even though I was constantly working 50+ hours a week. They could not afford to increase my wages, so I started to look for another job. In the September we went on a belated honeymoon which we were gifted. It was a small golf place in Kent where Tanya, Georgina and I could take a week away from Norwich to rest and explore if we wished. On one of the days we went over to France by ferry. On our return from the honeymoon our relationship started having issues again.

I was offered a job at Heatrae Sadia for more money, and having just completed a new brochure at work listing over 1200+ lamps, it was the right time to change jobs in the hope it would help life at home.

It was around this time my mum separated from her

fourth husband and moved into the bungalow next door to my grandparents which they also owned in Hellesdon.

The flat purchase went through in the December, two days before Georgina's birthday, and in with the mortgage I had included enough money to clear small debts I had and get new UPVC windows fitted to replace the Crittall single glaze council windows. The windows were fitted, but life between Tanya and I was not great. I did not like the arguments with Georgina around, so I went to stay with my mum to hopefully save our marriage by having some time apart.

At Tanya's request, I still went round daily to put Georgina to bed when I finished work, and late in the February I financially could not afford to live elsewhere while providing everything for the flat, so I had to discuss this with Tanya. After putting Georgina to bed I asked Tanya that we should talk, but this did not go down well and it turned into an argument as she did not like what I said. Things got heated, I was hit around the head and had things thrown at me. Georgina appeared at the door and I repeatedly asked Tanya to calm down. In a last effort I pushed her onto the sofa she was stood in front of. The next thing I knew, Tanya had grabbed Georgina while she was wearing only a nappy and tried to leave. Obviously I tried to make her see sense, it was cold outside, and as she went down the stairs, I tossed her a blanket. I gave myself a couple of minutes to calm down before getting in my car to find them. I found them waiting at a bus stop and wound my window down so I could try telling them to go home for Georgina's sake. A minute or so later one of Tanya's friends appeared saying there were police officers at the flat. I left them at the bus stop to return to the flat and speak to the police officers. When I got there, I was greeted by two male officers, one of which I asked to go and check Georgina was safe and warm after giving him brief details of the situation. The other officer and I went up to the flat where I told him my version of events while we both had a cigarette. Once I had finished, he told me this should all be dealt with quite simply. After a brief time we heard a knock on the door and upon opening I was met by the officer I had sent to check on Georgina. He promptly read me my rights and arrested me for ABH, which I found laughable after what I had just told the other officer and given the fact I had marks on me and blood coming from a scratch on my hand where she had tried snatching my keys before leaving. I locked up the flat and gave a key to one of the officers to go and give to Tanya. While walking to the police car I asked if I could retrieve some cigarettes from my car which I was left to do on my own while he opened the back door of the police car and in turn got into the passenger seat. I then got into the back of the police car after locking up my car. En route to the police station I was again told this should be wrapped up quickly and they were sure transport home would be organised. This was a whole new experience for me, never having been arrested before. As we entered the custody suite, I was greeted by two officers standing behind the desk who asked me to empty my pockets. This was not an issue until I remembered about the indecent pictures of Tanya I had, so I requested an envelope to put them in. The officer told me he had to view them but still retrieved an envelope for me. After looking at them, he laughed, which attracted the attention of the other officers who also asked to view them. I gave permission, it was her who had me arrested after all. I was also offered the chance to have Tanya arrested as I had sustained injuries. I turned this down as I wanted her there for Georgina as I was already in custody. I was shown to a cell where I had to remove my shoes before entering. I was asked if I needed anything and was told if I needed something at any time just to press the buzzer. The door was then closed while they organised the duty solicitor, and not knowing what was going to happen next I started doing sit ups and press ups to pass the time. After a while I wanted a cigarette and drink, so I pressed the buzzer. An officer came to check on me, and upon hearing my request went to the smoking cell and returned the occupant to their cell so I could use it. After my cigarette I was returned to my cell where a cup of water was waiting for me. A short while later I heard the door unlock and was informed the solicitor was here for me. I was moved to an interview room to talk with the solicitor, and I repeated to him the events of the evening. He told me that when it comes to the interview to repeat all I had just told him before I was returned to my cell. It was not long before I was collected for interview and returned to the interview room where I sat next to my solicitor and two officers sat on the other side of the desk. The tape was started and the interview began, but after a brief time the officer stopped the interview as there was an issue with the tape recorder, it had chewed the tape. Another tape was put in and we had to restart. After the interview I was returned to my cell and it was just a waiting game. A few hours later, following a delay due to shift change, they came to collect me and charged me with common assault, as I had said I pushed her onto the sofa, and given my bail conditions. One of these was that I was not to return to the road the flat was on and another to not contact Tanya personally. My belongings were returned to me and I was released at 02:00. This left me feeling lost as I was not able to retrieve my car from outside the flat. It was at this time I had to contact my dad for help. He came and collected me before taking me a couple of roads from the flat so he could collect my car without breaking my bail conditions.

On the first weekend I had Georgina we went to Snetterton market on the Sunday so we had different scenery to Norwich. I got a polaroid picture of us with an owl so she was always with me. I carried this everywhere.

I stayed at my mum's during this time, spending most of my free time at the pub where my brother worked in the kitchen, drinking Coke by the pint, and playing on the fruit machines. This was so that I had witnesses in case any further allegations were made against me saying I had broken my bail conditions. While all this was going on, I left Heatrae Sadia and started working shifts for a security company in Watton, a few miles out of Norwich. This was not necessarily my best choice, moving to a job that paid less, but it was a decision I made as I felt it would help my pending court case. While staying with my mum she introduced me to an online chat room on Freeserve, in the good old days of dial-up internet. The youth of today just will not understand the pain and frustration of waiting to connect to the internet. It was in one of these chat rooms that I started chatting to Mandy who lived just outside Salisbury on the edge of the New Forest. She invited me down for a weekend so I could get a break from the issues in Norwich and organised a B&B for me to stay in.

Even though Tanya insisted I kept regular contact with

Georgina this was made difficult by my bail conditions, so I had to get a third party to organise contact and collect her for me. I went to see a divorce solicitor, as having me falsely arrested was a step too far and I needed to ensure contact with Georgina continued. This was made easier after a month or so as Tanya moved out of the flat on the advice of her family. The area she moved to was not the greatest but at least I could now go and collect Georgina on my own without a third party being present as I could stop a short distance away and in view from the front door, even though I still needed a third party to organise it for me. Once Tanya moved out, I then had to apply to have my bail conditions changed so I could return to the flat I was paying for. I was eventually allowed to return, only to find the flat had been stripped of its contents, including the wall kitchen units and light fittings, I had been left with extraordinarily little that was of use and lots of rubbish.

I cannot recall exactly when, but during my stay at mum's, I returned one day after being out to find her on the floor. There was a smell of alcohol in the air and a couple of tablet bottles beside her. I managed to get a drunken/drugged response before using my mobile to contact an ambulance, my grandparents next door and then my sister, I could not deal with this alone. On the arrival of my grandparents, as I needed to give my brain time to decipher what I had walked into, I jumped in my car to go and collect my brother from his work, we had to deal with this as a family. On returning from collecting Andy, the ambulance and Lynn-Ann had arrived, my mum was being seen to, eventually the ambulance crew left with us being told to keep an eye on my mum, but she would sleep it off. What annoyed me the most; it was all over her boyfriend ignoring her.

CHAPTER 4

Mandy

I started visiting Mandy near Salisbury more, on the occasions when I didn't have Georgina, often travelling straight from my shift ending in Watton and returning just in time to start another shift. After a couple of months, I had the court case for the criminal matter and was given an 18-month suspended sentence. A month later, after the divorce hearing, including rebuilding my home with the basics so I could have Georgina to stay, the solicitors' fees and the payout I had to pay Tanya meant I was left with a debt more than £27k. I had to look on the bright side though, as I still had the flat and had cleared other debts nine months prior. Mandy and I were getting on well and with the amount it was costing in travel, we decided Mandy should move to Norwich and she found a job in a local care home.

I handed my notice in, joined a job agency and was lucky enough to get an offer of work straight away on the forklifts at British Sugar, working 8hr continental shifts for the winter season. There was always overtime available, so I often did 12hrs, and on the rare occasion a double shift. While working here I gained the nickname "biscuit", I assumed it was due to the ginger in my hair but found out afterwards it was due to me often taking a packet of biscuits for my lunch when I first started.

It was while I was working at British Sugar that Mandy swapped from working in a care home to care in the community like she did in Salisbury.

For my birthday that year Mandy got me a rally day at Brands Hatch. On the day I recall driving a silver Peugeot 206 and the tutor pulling the handbrake on the one from last corner, which caused me to start to spin out. On completion I found out I was close to the record lap time.

Once that contract finished, I applied for a job at The Russell Organisation which would be summer seasonal work in the warehouse. This was a company that provided event services to the likes of BMW, Mini, Vauxhall and Volvo to name a few. Even though my primary role was Goods-in Coordinator/Stores Assistant I was often used as the "get out of jail" card when they were short of event operators. This was due to my cheerful outlook and when approached by managers saying they had a problem, I always responded with "it's not a problem but an opportunity for me to succeed". This gained me respect and extra work in my spare time/ weekends when I did not have Georgina. Some of the events or trips I remember completing to save the day include:

- Working a normal Friday before driving a 7.5 tonne truck to a Volvo golf event at the back of Liverpool

Street station, London. Setting up that evening and staying in a hotel overnight before travelling back to Norwich the following day.

- On a Wednesday being asked to travel to Newcastle racecourse to take the replica Volvo touring car in a trailer, travelling down after work, getting a few hours' sleep in the vehicle before driving back.

- A trip to Brands Hatch for BMW as they had forgotten the merchandise. I was offered the chance to stay overnight but had to get back to see Georgina. I was told still to charge an overnight allowance.

- On a trip to Goodwood on behalf of Vauxhall team I was driving a van full of kit which broke down en route. The rest of the trip continued via a recovery truck; I slept in the BTCC motorhome over night before going to collect a hire car to drive home the next morning.

- The last-minute emergency call I received at 20:00 on a Friday from the Vauxhall team asking me to collect some stock from the warehouse and drive to Donnington racetrack for an event the following day.

- Another time, with all events personnel being out, I was asked to do a three-day event in Brindley Place, Birmingham for the Volvo team, where I was put up in a 4* hotel for the weekend. The bonus for me was that my presence was only required for set up and take down, but me being me I still attended the site each morning and evening to ensure the client was happy. The same client had another event a fortnight later in The Bull Ring, Birmingham and requested me as the operator again as they were so pleased on the earlier event.

While working here I was given the nickname of "Rigsby" as someone said I looked like him off the TV show "Rising Damp". When it came to an end-of-season night out, I wanted to look the part, so I dyed my hair and got hold of an old brown tank top to wear. To my surprise I was handed an envelope which contained a thank you card and some money as they had had a collection for me.

It was around this time that mum and her boyfriend moved over to Ireland, long enough to be allowed to get married, for which we travelled to Dublin. After a brief time, my mum returned and a short while later so did her husband, but their relationship had broken down, so they separated and got divorced.

I can't recall when in this relationship, but I do recall taking a trip to Lossiemouth, Scotland to visit Mandy's uncle and auntie. En route we spent a night with my second stepdad and his wife in Dumfries.

It was during this season while working at The Russell Organisation that I started doing "Kleeneze" to earn a bit of extra money. We upgraded my car to an automatic Peugeot 306 so Mandy could drive it too, but soon afterwards I returned home to find Mandy collapsed on the bathroom floor. She had no feeling below the waist and she was admitted into hospital. On admission they found she was a few weeks pregnant, and we were advised to have the pregnancy terminated (I look back now and am relieved). We were informed the numbness was due to past trauma and her brain had shut down her nervous system below the waist.

I took a week or so off for a deserved rest, and during this time received a call from the job agency asking if I'd be interested in returning for the sugar beet season. This was perfect timing, so I accepted and worked the winter season there again. As it was my second season, upon starting they taught me how to run the 50kg bagging plant and gave me a wage increase. A short while into the campaign, one icy morning en route to Cantley my vehicle slipped off the road straight through a telegraph pole, snapping it in half, and I ended up in a field. The car was written off and I replaced it with a Sierra estate, which my uncle converted to LPG for me to reduce running costs. Once the campaign finished, I contacted The Russell Organisation, who had rebranded as TRO, and they invited me back as a Vauxhall team assistant.

After a couple of months, I received a call from the agency saying they had had a call from British Sugar requesting me back with immediate effect, so due to the pay difference I returned. During the summer we worked standard day shifts. Mandy spent a lot of time in bed, saying she couldn't do much and as I was working a full-time position, running my Kleeneze business which was an established round passed down to me and doing all I could for Mandy (being her carer), I had very little time for myself, so I paid one of my Kleeneze customers to come round a couple of times a week and clean the flat for us. Several months passed and Mandy still wasn't doing much around the flat or helping me with my workload. I recall being in the car taking Georgina home after one of my weekends. Mandy had come for the drive to get out of the flat, and in conversation she told me of a dream she kept having about me telling her to leave and move back to Salisbury. I was asked if I would ever do that, I responded by saying can we discuss this once we've dropped Georgina off, and Mandy went extremely quiet. Once we dropped Georgina off, I was asked to elaborate. I told her how I felt that she should be improving and doing more around the house as I'd seen correspondence from the doctor that indicated things were improving massively. She responded, saying things had, but she just couldn't be bothered, so I gave her a month to prove to me she still wanted to be with me and start helping. Every day that following week I got home from work to a spotless flat, tea on the table and any Kleeneze bits that needed doing done ready for me to go out delivering the catalogues. Enough was enough, she had been taking advantage of me, so I told her I'd borrow a van from my family business, she could take anything she wanted from the flat and I was taking her back to Salisbury next weekend. It was agreed she would take most of the items in the flat including the furniture (I didn't object because the majority was purchased with her). On the evening before moving day, I packed the van, packed to perfection with no spare space, I couldn't even have squeezed another coat in the back if she'd had one (even the front seat had a box on beside her). Unfortunately, the only item not packed from her list was a microwave/combi oven. I drove her back to Salisbury, leaving early, unloaded everything and drove straight home.

CHAPTER 5

Helen

It was time to reset and restart, I needed time for me and to rebuild my home for Georgina. I spent a fair amount of my spare time online in chat rooms, but I did not want a woman in my life, I did not have spare money to be going out unless it was for work or while I had Georgina. After a while I started talking a lot to Helen who also lived in Norwich, but she had her own issues, so she very rarely left her house. We helped each other in many ways just by talking online. I guess she didn't think I was eating correctly as I returned home from work one day to find a box on my doorstep with some frozen home cooked meals in, some snacks for me and some girly gifts for Georgina. I realised who had sent the gift instantly as most of the bits were what we'd discussed the previous night, so I sent a message of thanks and asked why. The response made me happy, that someone who I had only spoken to could care and want to help me, it was like "if I could be there to help you, I would be. I got my mum to drop them off, so please accept these and I wish to send more each week". I joked and said something like "next you'll want to do my washing too", in response to which I was told to leave it outside and I'll get mum to collect and drop it back in a couple of days. Everything seemed a bit weird but who was I to complain, I was getting the best of both worlds, someone doing my cooking and washing but no physical woman to cause me issues and take advantage of me. After a couple of weeks, I was there when her mum turned up. I spoke with her and asked why. She told me that she was seeing improvement, it was making Helen happy that she could help me and for that reason she was happy to ferry the food, clothes, etc around, because I was doing more for Helen than I realised.

It was around this time that I moved my mum to Redditch to be with her boyfriend in a property they had purchased together. I went round my mum's the Friday night to load her belongings into a van and left in the early hours of the morning so I was there first thing to unload and returned the same day, stopping on the A14 to get a couple of hours sleep en route home.

My contract with British Sugar ended at the end of the next sugar beet season, around the same time Helen told me she was going to go back to work. I asked about meeting her but was told the same as before: "If it happens it happens, but I'm sorry I can't". I'd promised her when we first started talking that I would never intentionally meet her until she was ready, and it would be on her terms. To this day, this still stands, even though I do occasionally see her dad now (an ice-cream man). I obviously used to speak with her mum, but I have never tried to find her or meet her. I will forever be grateful for what Helen and her family did for me over this time.

During the 18 months of our internet friendship, we messaged daily, supported each other, shared ideas and dreams and regularly listened to music, one song Helen shared with me and we claimed as our song was 'Stigmatised' by The Calling. This song is about a person who is in love with their partner but is hesitant to pursue the relationship because of societal pressures and prejudices (stigma). The person questions whether they should give up on themselves and their beliefs to be together, or if they should fight for their love despite the challenges. The chorus then repeats the idea that they should embrace who and what they have, even if it means they will be stigmatised.

I joined a different agency which specialised in driving and found myself working for Allied Bakeries doing bread deliveries. I was sent out to learn several routes so I could be a relief driver. The hours were during the night/early morning which didn't bother me, but I kept a lookout for a daytime job.

CHAPTER 6

Dawn

It was while working here that I received a call from an old Kleeneze customer, Dawn, asking if I was still doing Kleeneze. We chatted on the phone, and she invited me round for a catch up when I finished the next morning as I was then getting ready for work. I was out learning the Lowestoft route that night, so when I finished work, I grabbed a couple of waste loaves and headed round to see Dawn. On arrival I handed over the bread and was offered some breakfast. I requested toast and a coffee as I knew there were money issues in the house. We sat on the sofa talking and I started drifting off. The next thing I knew, a couple of hours had passed, and I woke with a blanket over me with Dawn sat by my side and my hand on her leg. I was overtired and needed more sleep. I was offered the bed upstairs which I agreed to, but I did not expect her to join me. It had been a while, she was twelve years older, and I was not going to miss an opportunity. Before her kids came home from school, I went home to shower and chill before going to work later that evening. While at work that night I received another message from Dawn thanking me for the day and saying I am more than welcome round whenever I am free. Work went quiet with the agency for a short time, and I found a job with A&P Transport delivering incontinence pads/nappies around Norfolk. I enjoyed this work and there was a good bunch of fellow drivers. After a couple of weeks, I was contacted by the agency asking me to come back to Allied, so I decided to do both jobs. I used to finish a bread run and go straight to A&P and sleep for a couple of hours in the carpark before starting, and after work I'd get roughly four hours' sleep before going to work again at Allied. I recall one night while doing the Wisbech route I was driving towards the third camp on Stanta training area we used to deliver to, but I couldn't recall delivering to the previous two camps. The bread was not in the truck, so I must have delivered it. This is when I gave up A&P as the agency paid more.

Often after having Georgina for my weekend or on a Wednesday evening after taking her home, my heart hurt and I would go for a long drive instead of being alone or returning to Dawn's, on a few occasions finding myself on the M25.

I started seeing Dawn more when not working and we became a couple. She admitted to me she really struggled with money, and I helped where I could, ensuring there was food in the house for the kids (she had three boys and one girl, but two of the boys had moved out), and after a while it also came out that she had an issue with alcohol and regularly took amphetamines, which she started as a replacement to painkillers. The area she lived in was not great, and families nearby were often out in the front gardens drinking and socialising.

Dawn had not seen one of her older boys for a while, but she knew where he worked so we went to search for him. He was in a bit of a mess and needed to get out of where he was living, so I offered to let him move into my flat while he got himself sorted.

I remember after a few months Dawn and I had had a disagreement and I left the house to take time out. On returning a few hours later I pulled into her road and something hit the side of my car. I stopped, thinking it was kids, but instead I found Dawn in a drunken state. Unfortunately, a police car was driving past and saw her verbally abusing me and stopped to intervene. It was around this time that I tried amphetamines so I could try and understand why Dawn treated me and acted the way she did.

I can't recall exactly when, but my mum and her boyfriend moved back to Norwich and rented a bungalow in Hellesdon this same year.

After a year or so, work with the agency had dried up, so I started looking for alternative work and came across what looked like a suitable job with a London agency as an electrician's mate at a new data centre that was being built. I applied and got a start date a couple of weeks before Christmas. I turned up for the job, and once inductions were completed I was paired up with an electrician. While on a break my phone rang and it was the agency informing me that unfortunately the job I was there for wasn't required, but if I was willing there was a general labourer position available with an immediate start. Work is work, so I was happy to take the position. I spent most of my time clearing up after the various trades on site, often walking round with a backpack hoover.

I recall going to Asda to do the Christmas shop. I had an issue because my credit card was declined (I had maxed it out over the previous few months with lack of work) and my bank account was empty as I was still waiting for my first pay cheque, and we had to leave empty-handed. I went to see my nanny and granddad and borrowed some money so we could return for the essentials to get us through.

After the Christmas break I returned to work and during the first week back was offered a position installing the access flooring. I happily accepted and contacted the agency to quit the general labourer job, and the following day started with the flooring guys.

Around this time, I was at my flat again as things weren't great with Dawn and I was messaged saying she was en route to the shop, and it was so dark I guessed where she was so went to find her. As I pulled up I'd wound my passenger window down, offering for her to get in, she bent down and picked up a rock and threw it at me, it was a good shot and I was lucky I'd got the window down but it struck me on my head causing it to bleed. Because of the amount of blood, I left and went straight to A&E where they cleaned me up and glued the wound. As with other times I still returned to Dawn.

The following month, the Boss told me he was leaving the site as he was having issues getting money from who he was working for, but if I were willing to work the weekend he would pay me up to date with a little bonus as he needed to get the area he was on finished and collect all his tools. Fortunately, it was not a Georgina weekend, so I went in and helped him. On the Monday I still turned up even though I did not have an employer and was fortunate enough to be introduced to the new flooring team who came in and wanted me onboard as I knew the site.

I decided to sort my financial mess out and contacted my bank to see my best options. I surrendered my credit cards that were still maxed out and increasing monthly with charges. I ended up consolidating all my debts and put my mortgage on interest only payments to increase my cash flow.

Life with Dawn was not great, but I would not give up ensuring her kids were safe and looked after. There were often issues that required me to leave. I didn't want to go to the flat as her son was there, so I would sleep in my car so as not to be found. The relationship was not stable in the slightest. Dawn often spent all day in bed, and when I was not working I was often tidying/sorting the house out, including taking bags regularly to the laundrette for a service wash, due to the build-up of dirty laundry.

After a few months, the data centre was nearing completion, the other flooring guys left the site and I was left to make any adjustments or alterations that were needed by the electricians or installation engineers. A couple of guys wearing suits came over to talk to me about what my role was and my past working history. They then offered me a three-monthly rolling contract working for them self-employed while they migrated and installed all the servers. After more in-depth discussions I agreed and everything was looking up.

Life with Dawn was still having many difficulties, money was disappearing as fast as I earned it.

The agreement was that I worked when they needed me. Most of the work would be unsociable hours as server migrations would have to be done during the night and often at weekends, but they would give me a minimum of five shifts a week. I was also paid by the shift, not by the hour. I will always remember, shortly after I started, the new vans were outside and we were told to go and meet the big boss to fuel them up at Tesco. When I arrived, the boss was already filling his new Range Rover. I pulled up at the pump next to him and started fuelling up. After a short time, I swore and said these are unleaded aren't they (having a joke as I was filling with diesel) only to hear all the obscenities under the sun. You guessed it, he had only gone and filled up with unleaded instead of diesel, and with an 84-litre fuel tank this is quite a big mistake.

It got to the stage that Georgina occasionally didn't come at weekends if she knew we were at Dawn's, so it was decided that on Georgina's weekends we would go to the flat. While I was working at the data centre, on the rare occasion I was called to work, Georgina would come with me and sleep in the car in a secure compound. Not ideal, but protecting Georgina was my priority as she didn't want to go to Dawn's.

Working with this team was one of the highlights of my working career. I recall one time after we had finished all the server moves and decommissioned a data centre, we went to carry out a heat load test at a different data centre near Newcastle. It was scheduled so that we had the Wednesday off, so another transfer and migration was organised in Manchester. Unfortunately, there had been some issues, and we were required to do further testing. So once the tests were completed, we then still conducted the transfer, which made it an extremely long day. En route back to our hotel in the early hours, we received a message to add £500 to our invoice that week as a bonus. I was given a condition that I bought something for myself though, so I bought my first private vehicle reg M44 KDD.

It was around this time, during an argument with Dawn, I was leaving the house and she threw a candle in a glass or ceramic cup at me. It hit me an inch from my right eye, causing a cut (which scarred me) and in the following days a horrendous black eye. It wasn't long after this that I took Georgina on a last-minute unplanned trip to Disneyland by coach and we stayed in a hotel a short distance away.

Not long after the trip to Newcastle, my immediate boss offered me his Toyota Landcruiser, which he had owned since new, for a bargain price. This vehicle was previously his pride and joy and now it became mine, and without question has been my second favourite vehicle to date, and with the private plate on it didn't show its age. My current contract ended and I was offered a renewal but the work would be in Heathrow. Even though the money offered was good, I needed to be in Norwich for Georgina.

I remember one Christmas after I had evicted Dawn's oldest son from my flat, he turned up at the door and tried to cause a scene by starting on me. I put him to the floor as I was not interested in fighting with any of her children, and in the best possible way told him to disappear. I'm not sure if it was the same Christmas period or not, but during a disagreement with Dawn, I was in the kitchen and had what I thought was a cup thrown at me. I left soon after to get space and went to see my family and was told to get it checked. When I visited a walk-in centre, they advised me it was remarkably like a knife wound. I had had enough of this but felt I could not give up as someone needs to be there for her children. During the time I was with Dawn, my first call in difficult times or after being assaulted was to visit Georgina to get a hug. On a few occasions, Tanya also supported me and gave me strength.

I started working with a neighbour who fitted windows as he needed a labourer. Most of our work was away in Kent and Devon. Even though we went where the work was, I worked with him for four months which was not a terrible thing as it gave me time away from Dawn. I recall one of my last week's working with him. It was a busy week, Monday was pop to Colchester but his van's driveshaft broke en route, so the van needed sorting. We decided to load my vehicle with what was needed for the week's work. We left early for Northampton to conduct some window repairs. We finished there and I drove down to Davenport, getting there in the early hours, completed two full days' work and drove overnight on the Thursday back to Colchester to carry out the work we missed on the Monday. When it came to getting paid on the Sunday I only got four days, a bit cheeky since it was my vehicle that was used and I drove for two nights to ensure we completed all the week's work. We did not fall out as friends, but I decided working with him would end.

I joined another agency and got work at HDN as a courier. I enjoyed the work as it was challenging and I was kept busy. After three months working there I was offered an owner-driver's position, self-employed. I hired myself a van (BJ10 BYU) and took on the route I had been covering with the agency. Being self-employed had its benefits as we could take extra parcels and work longer every day. Another owner-driver and I employed another driver so we could take it in turns to do the Saturdays. Not long after I became an owner-driver, I came out of Dawn's one morning and found two of the tyres had been stabbed on the van (I had already learnt to carry two spares). We had an idea of who it was but I didn't have time to deal with it so just got on with my day. At work I got the nickname of "one sheet" from the office staff as I always had "plenty" of parcels but only ever asked for the sign-out sheet and not the full run sheets like everyone else did. When the time came for the catalogue campaigns, I would often claim extra areas and deliver them with Georgina so she could earn some pocket money. I would drive and she would run and post.

Shortly after starting with HDN, I decided to do a make it or break it move and emptied all my belongings from my flat into Dawn's, so I could get it sorted to rent or sell as it was wasted money sat there empty most of the time.

By the December, I decided I'd had enough of the issues from being with Dawn and I wanted out. I was working a minimum of twelve hours a day but often fifteen, so I'd ensure the kids had a Christmas to remember (I got them all a TV each for their bedrooms). I recall coming home from work on 30th December to be asked what we were doing for New Year. I had it all planned in my head and responded with "I don't know what you're doing, but I am loading all Georgina's stuff, my work bits and all my clothes and leaving". Surprisingly, this did not go down well. On the first of January I drove away from Dawn's with my van loaded and went straight to see my dad, out of Norwich so I could not be hassled.

Over the next few weeks, I started to rebuild my flat again and was determined to make it a proper bachelor's pad. I had giant leather bean bags as seats which I also slept on, a 50" 3D television on the wall, a blue-ray DVD player and the dogs of a surround sound system, the cooker was never wired in from when I last fitted the kitchen, but I did have a microwave to cook in. I never bothered with a bed as that was a cost I could postpone. I was living on tinned spaghetti bolognaise (19p) and tinned custard (11p) and I would eat straight from the tin to save washing up or heating costs, so when Georgina came I had the money to take her out and for takeaway, even though she often had the same as me, which was her choice. In the February, Dawn contacted me as she had found out she was pregnant. I wasn't willing to take her word on it without proof, so I waited for an ultrasound scan. I started popping in once a week just to check on Dawn's condition and that things were ok.

Around this time, HDN joined forces with Yodel, and after six months of hiring a van I decided to buy myself a new Citroen Relay (AO11 CHG). Work was getting busier and I often offloaded some of my parcels to a friend to deliver. Apart from the weekends or times I was using my Landcruiser, it was parked at my flat. Well, that was until one day when working I had a call from the police telling me my vehicle had been found burnt out in a different part of the city. That was all I needed, extra hassles of dealing with insurance companies and DVLA. I got my number plate transferred to my van and eventually got a payout from the insurance company, not what I had paid for it but close enough.

As time passed, I could tell Dawn was looking after herself better and I started visiting more regularly. As her due date approached, I was popping in most days and occasionally staying the night. I recall the night before Connor was born, we had a massive argument and I was told she didn't want to see me again. Guessing it was her hormones, I contacted Dawn the following morning and ended up inviting her to come out with me while I was working. I didn't mind as I knew I passed several medical centres if anything was to happen. After the deliveries were all done and we had returned to the depot to offload the returns, Dawn asked me to take her to the maternity suite, and Connor was born at 20:53. As it was Dawn's fifth child, we were able to leave the hospital that evening, The next day, we popped in to see Georgina so she could meet her brother and I started to move some of my clothes back into Dawn's.

Over the next couple of months, the tensions between Dawn and myself started to increase, but I was there to ensure Connor had what he needed primarily, as well as making sure his siblings were ok. Dawn had quit the alcohol and amphetamines, so it was not that that was causing the issues. Dawn would ensure Connor was looked after, but she spent a lot of time lying on the sofa and was getting his siblings to do the tasks around the house when I was at work.

When Connor was about ten months old, Dawn told me to leave during an explosive argument saying, "You are only here because of Connor. If you want to see him again, best you see a solicitor". Obviously, the next day I went to the solicitors to get the access arrangements in place. Things were very tense, but I made sure things were organised and agreed quickly for Connor's safety. Not that I thought Dawn would intentionally hurt him, but so that I could ensure Connor had stability through contact with me as his siblings' fathers weren't on the scene.

I moved back to my flat again. My dad talked about coming over to see me and staying the night so he could have a drink, so I went out and brought a bed and bedding. I also chose to go back to my tinned diet to build my money up.

In the August, our depot moved to join the other Yodel depot, and I joined a consortium with five other owner- drivers so we were not stuck doing the same route all the time. Our area covered most of North Norfolk and we would do a month and then switch routes. By doing this, we got regular weekends off, after six or so months the consortium separated, and looking back I feel some of the other drivers weren't sure about the route they wanted and where they could earn the most money. I was left with the Fakenham route, which covered quite a large area.

CHAPTER 7

Angie

In the December, I started chatting regularly to a woman in the office called Angie (who was also at college studying Photography). She was 18 years younger than me, and this obviously caused issues with Dawn when she found out, even though at the time we were just friends. Several solicitors' letters turned up with demands about having another woman around Connor. I've always been open and honest with my children, so when things between Angie and myself looked as though they may progress, I made sure I talked it through with Georgina to get her opinion, as their age gap was only three years. Her response was "I just want you to be happy". So I introduced them to each other along with Angie's sister who was the same age as Georgina. Everything went well and Georgina was happy, so we started seeing each other more and dating.

It was around this time that I had an accident in my van, colliding with a builder's van parked up on the side of the road in Burnham Market. I knew it had done some serious damage as it ripped the wing off and the tyre was shredded. I swapped the wheel over and continued my route. Having phoned the Citroen dealership they told me to take it to them and they would loan me a van until the insurance company dealt with it, so when my working day ended I dropped my van off and collected the loan van. After a few weeks, my insurance company wrote my van off, so I organised buying another new one, and the dealership allowed me to continue using the one they loaned me until mine arrived. With the crazy amount of hours I worked, I struggled to get time to get my private plate off as I had to visit a DVLA office, and when I eventually got in they refused to refund my twelve months' vehicle tax, which I'd purchased early as I didn't have an assessor's letter. This in turn meant that I couldn't retain my personal plate.

My new van arrived the following month (AO13 LBA). Angie was staying over from time to time and my life was changing for the better. Her family all approved of me; my life seemed on the up. I knew that September was a bad time for her, so I wanted to do something special. Before I did, I went to see her grandma and grandpa to seek their approval regarding me asking for her hand in marriage. They approved, so I started organising a trip to Disneyland Paris. I was fortunate enough to book the week trip with her most negative day being on the Wednesday. With Angie being what I believed to be my reward and happiness, I gave her all she wished for in material objects so she would feel special and wanted.

Her college year was ending, and with our life being good together I invited her to move in when her course finished on the condition she continued with her plan of going to university. She was accepted by a few but she decided Norwich University of the Arts was the most suitable. Her condition was that I got the cooker wired in. In the summer, Angie moved in, bringing only clothes as previously she had been living with her grandparents, and she started adding her own little feminine touches to the flat.

Our holiday week came. Angie knew we were going, so on the Monday we got a train to London and then changed to a direct train to Disneyland, where we stayed in one of the on-site hotels. My plan was, travel Monday, park Tuesday, Paris Wednesday, park Thursday and travel home Friday. So when we got there we went exploring around the village to get some food before settling down for the night. We got up quite early, had breakfast and headed into Disneyland, rushing round to get on as many rides as possible. That evening we stopped in the village for food before heading back to the hotel for an early night. On the Wednesday morning, we had breakfast before getting a coach into Paris. Angie was dressed in clothes she thought was suitable and fashionable but in my eyes she looked like a French tart (I did tell her about my thoughts towards the end of the day). But I wasn't going to let it affect my plans. We got to the centre of Paris, Angie with camera in hand, and started exploring. Me being me, I preferred the back roads to the main routes and we visited many attractions before arriving at the Eiffel Tower. Angie isn't keen on heights so it took me a good half hour to convince her that going to the top for pictures would be worth it. Eventually I talked her into it and we got the lift to the top, Angie was amazed at the views and started taking photos instantly so I popped to get a couple of drinks before returning. Then, a little nervous,

I dropped to one knee and proposed with a ring from my pocket. Angie was gobsmacked, burst into tears and said YES! When we returned to Disneyland we headed to the village to celebrate at the Chicago Rock Café for food and a few bars after for drinks. En route back to the hotel Angie threw up in a flowerbed (a humorous memory of our first night of being engaged). On the Thursday, we visited the studio park and had an early night after the eventful day earlier, and on the Friday we travelled home. Angie was in shock at the amount of people who were aware and helped me to make it a memorable holiday to block out the pain the date held previously. I was not in a rush to get married after earlier experiences and told Angie it would not be before she had finished university.

Work was starting to get busy, with peak period imminent. I was working long hours and due to commonly being last back I often phoned ahead and as my apology would take cheeseburgers from McDonalds for any office staff still working. I was earning good money and life was so much happier.

Unfortunately, in mid-October en route to Fakenham, I had to swerve to avoid rear ending a car and hit a tree stump on a grass verge. I didn't realise it at the time but this cracked the front cross member on impact. I called the office, who sent an agency guy out to me with the instructions that he was to drive, and due to the quantity of parcels and size of my route I had to accompany him as the agency normally only did clear ups (forty-fifty parcels in a small area, I had roughly one hundred and thirty on board). When he arrived, we transferred the parcels and agreed we would get my van to the dealership before doing the route. I could drive it but it only managed three of the ten miles before giving up the ghost. He then towed me the rest of the way. We set off on the route and had delivered about ten parcels when I explained to him the difference between me driving and him driving, i.e. 20:00 or 23:00. The agency guy did well that day, and by the end of it decided he would investigate becoming an owner-driver too. A month later, he took on his own route.

I could not afford to buy another van and knew my insurance would be astronomical on the next renewal since I had written off two vans within six months. I had renewed my insurance in the August so I still had several months left on my current policy. So I hired a van on a long-term deal.

My mum got married this year for the sixth time, I can't even say it's because of the cake as there wasn't one. This was just a quiet wedding with only immediate family attending, with a meal afterwards at a pub in Drayton.

It wasn't long after Christmas when I was contacted by Social Services as they had concerns about Connor and his siblings. They had been put on the child at risk register and Social Services asked for a meeting with me. At the meeting they told me they wanted me to go for full custody of Connor. I told them he could move in immediately, but I didn't have the funds to pay solicitors' fees, as the last occasion had cost me significantly a couple of years previously. I was told there was no need to worry as I had their backing, but they would need to do it through the proper channels.

I can't recall when, but I believe it was around this time that Angie decided to learn to drive and I bought her a car at auction. One of the times I went out with her, she panicked, forgot to brake, and hit a brick wall and bent the bonnet. No one was injured and these things happen, so I purchased a second-hand bonnet and replaced it.

I had to give Yodel three months' notice, so in the May I handed my notice in so my contract with them ended when my insurance ran out in the August. This would also tie in with the court case scheduled in the October.

I caught up with Paul, an old school friend, a couple of weeks before I ended with Yodel. He owned a building company and offered me some work while the custody cases were going on, driving for and working with a carpenter who was recovering from a leg injury, and we spent most of our time doing repairs at schools. Paul also organised a VW music festival called Dubs at the Hall (DATH), and he invited us to attend and join the crew.

Once I had left Yodel, Angie wanted out as well and when I saw an advert for a local restaurant walking distance from the flat, she applied and got the job as a waitress which fitted around her NUA timetable. Now in her second year, she was wanting to quit but was given the opportunity of a week in New York at a discounted price in the February, so I told her if I paid for the trip she could think about her future while away, and if she still wanted to quit afterwards I would support and accept her decision, knowing I had done all I could to help her continue in her planned career.

One weekend when we had Connor, Angie was leaving for work at 11:00 and asked me to remind her to get the car washed next week. Connor and I were due to go to the local park, so before we went I thought we would go and get the car washed to surprise Angie and save her a job. As we were driving round the ring road, I saw flashing blue lights behind us and realised I was being pulled over. I pulled in and wound down the window. The policeman said to me "You don't look like an Angie". I told him she was my partner and what had happened, including that I had a vehicle until two months previously. He worked out that I did not have insurance so because of this and the fact that Connor was with me he radioed for another officer to collect Angie to drive the vehicle home and issued me a ticket for no seatbelt and no insurance, I attended a drivers' awareness course for the seatbelt and had heard nothing about no insurance. I waited six months so as not to raise awareness and then insured myself on Angie's car. It was fortunate that during the time I did not have a vehicle. Paul gave me use of a company vehicle.

Several meetings were attended with social workers, and a month before the custody court case I found out Connor had been removed from the child at risk register, which in turn meant that his social worker changed. The new social worker did not seem keen on me getting Connor, and when it went to court I told the judge he had reports from various sources including my own (I wasn't allowed to mention siblings), but since the court proceedings had started Dawn had improved - shock horror. I didn't get custody, but what made it worse was, as we left the court the social worker said to me "it won't be many years before Connor will be residing with you". A month or so later I found out that Connor's sister had been removed from the home and placed into foster care, but Connor was able to stay as he had regular contact with me.

I reported back to Paul, who was pleased in a way that I did not get custody, as he valued me as an employee and offered me further work.

It was around this time, at Angie's grandma's wake, that I was talking with someone who invited me along to Soul church. I had heard of Soul Church, as Jon who I'd known as a teenager was the lead pastor there, and when I heard that he had taken it on I had thought about checking it out. I attended the following week and it felt like Jon was talking directly to me, so after the service I spoke with Jon who prayed with me, and I asked God back into my life. Looking back over my life I felt He had not actually ever left me since the first time but He just guided my route even with the bad decisions I made. My thinking is, in my early years I fell in with the wrong crowd so He withdrew me. I joined the Army so He gave me the option to leave. He introduced me to Tanya so I could assist her torn background, but when I struggled He pulled me out. With Mandy, he knew I could cope with her problems but when she took advantage He gave me the strength to end it, putting Helen in my life to support me but also using me to assist her in her recovery from her trauma. I chose to have a relationship with Dawn, in which He would use me to protect the children and help her to quit her addictions, but He could use the knowledge I gained to assist others later in my life and so helped me to end the relationship when I had been taken advantage of too often, and at the time I felt Angie was my reward for all I'd been through.

Work was slow and I received a call from Yodel offering me peak work, so after discussing with Paul I agreed to go back for a few weeks with the bonus of using their van and fuel but still earning good money. After the Christmas, I was struggling to find work so I posted on Facebook. Paul contacted me and offered to hire me back but as a sub-contractor. I was happy with this, so I returned. In the February, Angie went off on her week to New York which I hoped would encourage her to stay to finish her degree. Unfortunately, on her return she still wanted to quit, which she did and began working full-time rather than part-time at the restaurant.

I was introduced to David at Soul Church who was also part of the Safety team. He was also ex-forces, we became good friends and bounced off each other when needed.

In the June, I clearly remember getting a call from my dad to inform me that my grandad had passed away. I wasn't far from Norwich airport and after being told I sat there for 5 minutes or so just taking in what I had just been told. I guess it was made easier by already knowing he was not in the best way and already in hospital, I know I would have attended the funeral, but I can't remember it. RIP grandad.

We worked DATH again that year but I was asked to co-ordinate the facilities team. Since I didn't have a team, I asked Georgina and a couple of her friends along to help.

A large group from Soul Church were going to the Hill-song Conference at the O2. I couldn't go for the full 3 days as I had work booked in, but I finished the job I was doing on the Friday morning, jumped in my car and headed down for the last evening while Angie was at work.

In the October, I recall being informed by my mum that grandad had been taken to hospital, so I left work to join my mum at the hospital. I believe for a couple of days I visited daily. Then one morning I received a call first thing telling me there wasn't long. I got to the hospital to find my mum already there and her brothers or my siblings were still to arrive. I went in to grandad, had a chat with him and gave him a shave so he was ready for his other visitors. A couple of days later, after most had visited, grandad went to sleep for the last time. RIP Grandad.

Towards the end of the year, when browsing Facebook I came across a discounted wedding due to a cancellation, so I booked it for the following year. The deal I booked included the service, wedding breakfast and evening reception all at the same venue. I knew Angie wanted to get married at Brundall church though, so I enquired with the vicar to see if the church would be available, and luckily it was.

I left most of the wedding planning to Angie but made sure I stayed in the loop with plans. Using my contacts I gained some good deals for the things she wanted i.e., an ice-cream van, bouncy castle, fireworks.

The night before the wedding, I stayed at my best man's house and he drove me to the church, picking Connor up en route as he was my ring bearer, having a drink in the pub opposite the church, passing the time and waiting for the guests (I only had a coke as I did not want a repeat of my last wedding). I had arranged with a friend to collect Angie in his split screen VW camper and to be our wedding transport. After the ceremony we had the normal photos before getting into the camper to go to the reception venue. The rest of the day went well. It was made incredibly special by having friends and family around us to help celebrate. Angie's wedding present from myself was a personal plate MR54 DKN (MRS A DKN). We had a mini moon after the wedding, travelling around the UK for a week.

Even though I no longer worked for Paul, he contacted me to see if we would be interested in working DATH again that year. We did, as we both enjoyed the VW scene and had previously gained many friends within the VW community.

We went to Tenerife a couple of months later for our honeymoon, staying in a 4* hotel all-inclusive, paid for with the money we were gifted at our wedding, flying in and out of Norwich airport for convenience.

For my birthday I got my own private plate (MR04 DKN) to match Angie's, which I put straight on my car.

Early the next year, Jon the Pastor from Soul Church contacted me to ask if I'd coordinate the safety team. With my knowledge and experience it made good sense, so I agreed with a couple of conditions: David was to be my 2ic, I could change the name, and I could choose who I had on team. I changed the name to Venue Team as it sounded less intimidating. Over the 18 months I ran the team, I increased the number of volunteers that consisted of ex- and serving military, homeless, business owners, a mental health nurse, schoolteachers, un-employed and retired people serving to keep the congregation and kids safe. After a couple of months, the church sent me to get my SIA badge to aid and improve my knowledge, in view of the growing threat of terrorism for the church.

It was around this time I won a competition run by Jet fuel stations. I was fortunate enough to win fuel for a year, well at least that is what the competition stated. It was a gift card with £1000 credit. I had never won anything like this before and being me I used it all in a couple of days short of three months. Not all on myself though. I had massive pleasure in filling my own car or Angie's and then paying for the random person behind me. I was often thanked by the recipient but on a couple of occasions I was met with tears of happiness and told it meant they now had money for food as they had chosen fuel so they could get to work to earn. I will never forget one elderly lady I blessed who just stood there in shock as she couldn't understand it and told me that was the nicest thing anyone had ever done for her.

David from Soul Church bought me a ticket for the Hillsong Conference at the O2 and I ended up driving one of the minibuses down to save the interns the travel costs. This didn't cause any issues and we stayed in a hotel a short tube ride away. I also drove a minibus to Bradford to ferry some of the youth to their summer camp when they were a driver short the following month.

I was feeling content and everything was going good for us, so I decided to put the flat on the market after owning it for fifteen years (my safe place: I had kept it through all my trials and tribulations). While we were looking for our perfect home, we came across a house on the road I was born on, but it was slightly over our budget. Angie and I decided we would have a joint mortgage and split the bills fifty/fifty. Upon viewing, it was ideal, three bedrooms, a walk-through garage, a small garden, drawers in the stairs, only the kitchen needing replacing (the same layout as the house I was born in). I put an offer in and received a counteroffer which I accepted. I saw an advert for The Bull PH in Hellesdon as it was under new management so recommended that Angie should apply as it would be closer to our new home. She did and was given a supervisor role.

My flat sold for the asking price and I fortunately already knew someone living on the new road we were moving to, so I was able to fill his garage before we moved into our new family home in the November.

We moved in, and for the first few months I topped up the joint account where we had shortfalls with the bills, until I was struggling and had to ask Angie to increase her payments.

David and his wife were moving to Orkney and needed some work done on their new property, so with my driving experience I also moved their belongings in a 7.5 tonne truck. We loaded the truck on a Saturday and I left that evening. It was dark and I stopped for a sleep in the cab near Dumfries and got my head down for a few hours. When I woke, I realised where I was so stopped in for a coffee with my old stepdad before carrying on to Aberdeen to catch the ferry to Kirkwall. I stayed the week and carried out some maintenance before returning empty on the Friday morning by ferry from Stromness – Thurso, witnessing some amazing views and scenery and only stopping for a couple of hours in Newcastle to see my stepmum.

Angie and I both went along to the Hillsong Conference, staying at an Airbnb a couple of tube stops from the O2.

After being in our new home for nearly a year, we also decided to replace the kitchen. Fortunately, we saved a fitting fee as I carried out the work myself.

In the October, Georgina moved into a new build with her boyfriend and told me they weren't the only one's moving in. A few weeks later when Angie and I went round for tea they announced Georgina was pregnant. Even though I already knew, I openly expressed my concerns regarding them being young and due to my own past knowing how difficult this was, I was apprehensive for our drive home knowing what statements and questions I would be getting from Angie as she had expected to be pregnant before Georgina. As expected, things, got heated in the car on the way home. Once home I went for a walk to clear my head and ended up sleeping in the car on the drive.

I stood down from my voluntary position with the Soul Church Venue Team when they brought in someone above me whose team management approach I did not feel would work within the church and the volunteers I had on team.

I was getting plenty of work with my own private jobs, and in the April I was contacted by one of my customers offering me his VW T5 for an exceptionally good price. Obviously, I bought it, as I had always wanted one. A couple of weeks later I was contacted and offered a fulltime position looking after a marina and some holiday cottages. I took the position as I wanted some security and regular money without the stresses of continuously hunting for work.

On our first wedding anniversary, Angie had booked a weekend away, and while we were away she said she wanted a new car. So on our return we went to Audi and I ended up putting a deposit down on a brand new Q2, but we put the finance in Angie's name. We sold the Golf after putting the plate on retention but Angie did not want it on the Audi Q2.

In the months after buying my van, I spent money doing it up and converting it on a budget to a basic camper van while still wanting to use it as a work van. I'd also taken up running, even if it were only the 5k parkrun on a Saturday in the beginning.

Angie and I both went along to the Hillsong Conference

again that year but this time we shared a room with friends at a youth hostel.

It was around this time that Chris from the Venue Team at Soul Church invited us to join his family on Mildenhall base for a day to experience base life, Angie was working, as she often was, so just Connor and I went. The most memorable part for me was when we met his wife, who was working ground control, and we got to have a look on a C130 plane prepping to leave. Connor then got to direct the same plane before it took off back to America.

Things between Angie and myself started to change, she was working a lot and was spending more time out with friends. I didn't believe it, but I did consider the possibility of her having an affair with someone at work.

I started running more in the evenings to avoid spending time alone at home, Angie had mentioned wanting a new Apple watch for her birthday to help her at work, so I bought one and gave it to her on purchase so she could get use of it straight away.

Things between us were not right. Two weeks later when I got home from work, she was sitting in the dark. She told me she had fallen out of love with me and wanted to break up. I talked her into going for a meal so we could discuss and try and resolve this. I was heartbroken. During the meal, she said she needed to go to her mum's, and because she had been drinking, I said I would take her. I sat outside for several hours before she came out and told me she would come home to try and resolve our situation.

We got home and went to bed in silence. I could not sleep, so after a couple of hours I got up and went for a drive (not the best idea given my state of mind) and ended up at Phil's (a friend) house knowing he got up early for the gym. We had a good chat. I went straight to work as I started at 08:00 and needed to keep my mind busy. I spoke to my boss when he arrived, and he offered to let me go home, but I needed to keep busy so I said I would stay and he told me to do what I thought best, but if I needed time out to take it.

Early in December I made the final payment on the debt that I'd had since first buying my flat. I'd increased it several times over the years but for the first time in over twenty years I was officially debt free, and touch wood I will never have the need for another loan.

The next couple of weeks were not good. I went out running most nights to keep myself occupied, at nighttime I was struggling to sleep and so was having an extra-large JD to help myself get to sleep.

Angie only spent a couple of nights at home, which was the weekend I had Connor. She said she was at her nan's, and when she was at the house there was little chat, but I got her to agree to be there for her birthday, so I did all I could to make it the best.

I woke early and cooked her breakfast in bed, ran her a bubble bath, passing the time waiting for a flower delivery, went to see Georgina and our granddaughter as I knew this was necessary. We then went out to The Hoste - Burnham Market for lunch before driving round the coast to Kings Lynn as I knew she wanted to visit some shops. We then drove back to ours as her friend was meeting us to go out for a meal. We left early so I could take them to see the Christmas lights as I knew it was one of her loves, only to be told I was wasting my time as she was not in the mood. We then met with her family for cocktails (I had a Coke) and a meal at Turtle Bay. After the meal we drove her friend home to Stalham and on the way home I was told it was her worst birthday and I had spoiled it by not allowing her to do what she wanted, which was to not be with me. We got home, and after a short time Angie left in her Q2, under the influence of alcohol.

I spent many occasions at silly o'clock sat outside in the street crying and trying to release the frustrations that had built up inside.

Over the next couple of weeks, she only returned home once or twice, while I was at work or when I had Connor, saying she was staying at her nan's. But her nan phoned me asking if I had heard from her, which did not help the state of my mind. She popped into my work on Christmas Eve before going to work herself, to ask if I could wrap the presents that she had for friends and told me she had Connor's presents in her car. It was my year to have Connor for Christmas, so when I finished work I collected Connor and returned home to wrap the presents.

Angie returned home from work in the early hours of Christmas morning. When Connor woke up, we went down-stairs to open the presents. Angie was due to leave for work again in a couple of hours but unsurprisingly there was noth-ing under the tree for me and only a couple of presents for Connor (neither of which were from us). I was not impressed as she had said she had Connor's presents and I told her if she did not want to be here to go. She rushed upstairs in her dressing gown to grab her work gear so I followed begging her to stay as I should not have said what I said. She left, still in her dressing gown. I had arranged to do parkrun with my mum, so I called her to come and collect Connor so I could drop Angie's family's presents off and join them later. I was angry and frustrated and should not have driven like I did, but I dropped the presents off, only to be asked why I physically threw her out. I hadn't, but I was not in the right frame of mind to talk about it, so I just left without saying a word and went to join Connor and the family at the parkrun.

Connor and I had previously been invited to join Phil and his family for Christmas lunch as Angie was at work, so after the parkrun we went there. Connor and I went home in the evening and Angie's grandad dropped our presents off on Boxing Day morning before I took Connor home. I did not see or hear from Angie even though she did visit the house while I was at work, collecting some personal clothes/items and removing several items from our shelves and sideboard (Emma Bridgewater and limited-edition Disney DVDs). I really struggled this following week, lots of long drives (which wasn't wise given how my head was), struggling to sleep but refusing to drink to numb the pain, often outside during the night considering if I should jump in front of the next car that passed. Fortunately, though, I had to pop into work for a couple of hours each day to service the hot tubs, plus my children and grandchild kept me grounded.

On New Year's Eve morning I received a message from an old friend who had joined the army the same time as me. We don't speak regularly but will always be brothers when needed. He asked if all was ok, I told him Angie had left and I was a mess. He told me to put the kettle on as he was on his way. When he arrived, we talked in depth, and he set me straight and sorted my head out over the five hours or so he was round. Before he left, he asked me what my plans were as he knew me being alone wasn't an option.

I had several invitations from different people for New Year's Eve, so I guess they were concerned for my wellbeing. I opted to join Chris (Venue Team) and his family on Mildenhall air base to see in the new year in American style. We had a meal and then went bowling. I dealt with everything ok until the last few strikes of the bell, and then I just broke down in tears. I excused myself and drove home. On the hour or so drive home, I decided enough was enough and that Angie and I were over.

CHAPTER 8

Katie

On New Year's Day in the afternoon, I received a message from Katie who I knew from church, asking if everything was ok as she had seen a couple of Facebook posts that concerned her. I told her what had happened and we started messaging each other. She was away visiting family, but after listening to me she offered to come round on her return and help me go through and sort out Angie's belongings. I admit I was ruthless when sorting through her things, binning more than I should have, but any valuable or personal memory items I piled up for Angie to collect. Emotionally Katie was of massive support and feelings started to grow between us.

In mid-January I went with my stepdad to Greece to crew a 24hr race he was running for five days. I needed to get away for my own personal strength, but it did also grow my feelings for Katie. On returning to the UK, Katie and I started seeing each other as a couple. I would sometimes spend time at hers, or occasionally we would stay at mine. I needed to be careful as I was still legally married, a fair few items I needed gone from the house went to hers as they were too valuable to get rid of.

As Katie's car was on its last legs, I insured Katie on my car as I had my van to use. Katie then had her car scrapped as she had my car to use. I had also put MR54 DKN on my car and MR04 DKN onto my van.

At the end of January I lost my job. The reason given was that my mind was not on my work and I was not performing to a satisfactory standard. It is what it is. I went to church the following morning and bumped in to one of my old customers who offered me some work renovating a bungalow he had for sale. I took the job and employed Katie's son as my labourer.

I'd entered for the Valentine's 10k. This would be my first race and I said I would run it for Katie's daughter who was going for an operation. I had only been for a run a couple of times since getting back from Greece, so I did not expect to run well. I decided to run with someone I knew from parkrun so I could use him as my pacer, as I knew he had been running for several years. With roughly 3k to go, I felt good and started to break away from him and I decided just to go strong for the finish line. I recall a marshal on a bike coming beside me to ask about my top (Athens 24hr). I exchanged a few words and passed him my phone for the sprint finish. I finished in 52.58 according to my Garmin watch. I got my medal and took it round to give it to Katie's daughter. After this, Katie and I became distant. She refused to see me even though her son worked with me until the end of February. I don't know what happened between Katie and I, obviously a relationship wasn't on her agenda, so as always I was left confused and concentrated on my work and immediate family.

The last time I saw Katie was at the beginning of March when I went to watch her son's first singing gig in Wroxham. I hadn't seen her for the two weeks prior. Katie still had my car, which I wasn't too bothered about as I'd paid the tax and insurance anyway and I was using my van. I hoped in time we could fix whatever had gone wrong. My car was returned a couple of weeks later after her son's car was repaired.

I had applied for a Quickie Divorce online and sent the signed paperwork off at the post office on my mum's birthday after doing a family parkrun and before going to do security at a boxing event in Ipswich for an old friend. I was looking forward to it, but as normal when I work security at events, nothing interesting happened that enabled me to release tension and stresses.

I finished renovating the bungalow on 21st March and just had to go and collect my tools and do the final clean up on 23rd. That evening, Covid-19 lockdown was announced. I went straight to see Connor before it started. The following day was my birthday, and I was stuck on my own, going mad. I was fortunate enough that Georgina and her partner were both key workers and I was needed to go and sit with my granddaughter for short periods while they crossed over between work. The next morning, I got a call asking me to cover security at a Co-op store in Long Stratton for a couple of weeks. The money was poor, but at least I would be out doing my bit to keep people safe and more importantly reduce the spread of Covid. When I started on the Thursday morning, everything seemed very strange, but I soon got things into an order I could control.

Even though I'd suffered minor bouts of Anxiety on occasions during my life, it was always something I'd found a way to deal with. I was finding it harder to process and some things just didn't make sense. If I was working or my mind was occupied with a task (often doing things for others), I was 100% fine, but when it came to going shopping for myself I really struggled. It often took me 30 mins plus just to leave the house to go and get a few bags of Kiev balls that I was living off at the time. This didn't make sense to myself as I could work security dealing with thousands of people. But a simple task really did affect me.

Within a couple of days of starting, the boss contacted me saying he needed somewhere to live as he didn't feel comfortable returning to the old chap he was living with; I was cautious due to the previous time he stayed with me, but I allowed him to stay at mine with conditions. A couple of weeks after moving in, he was disturbed by Katie returning some of my belongings along with my house key.

It was during my time working here that I joined a group called Single Pringles on Facebook so I could interact with people and have some sort of social life outside of work during these unknown times we were living in. I was also added to a Facebook group called MEN-TAL.K and after a short time was made an admin. This group was extremely beneficial especially in the current climate. I still am an admin, but the group hasn't taken off in the way we hoped it would.

I was working 07:00–15:00, seven days a week, and after work I would go shopping for those who were classed as high risk and vulnerable. I was also lucky enough to be working at a shop so I could get items for family and drop them off while collecting baking that was done for me. I also blessed many emergency workers who visited the store while I was working by paying for their shopping, but more importantly during this time I also learnt to love myself again and deal with my demons. It was during this time that I renewed my SIA badge for another 3 years. I ended up working fifty-five days without a day off. It was on the Wednesday I finally took off that I was told I would be finishing on the Friday.

That weekend, I spoke with Soul Foundation about offering my services. For the next few weeks I drove daily to collect pallets of food from Fareshare in Ipswich.

CHAPTER 9

Anne-Marie

During these times, I was commenting regularly on the Single Pringles Facebook group, which in turn made me a couple of new friends. I was not wanting a relationship but needed a friendship circle where I could talk openly about how I was feeling. Due to Covid, we used to have a Friday night social on Zoom, where we would all be in our own homes and having various chats just as if we were out at a local pub without leaving our own homes. Since I was still active with security/voluntary work, I regularly sat in my bedroom eating tea while on the Zoom call. The majority would be sat with alcoholic drinks but I stayed off the alcohol in case I was needed somewhere and had to drive.

I often spent my evenings in my back garden with a small open fire in the firepit. I'd been on the phone to my stepmum who had told me that things weren't good, she was struggling with her health. This was the occasion I first exchanged messages with Anne-Marie. I wasn't in my normal frame of mind so I was sitting with a glass of JD and Coke. I had looked at Anne-Marie's profile before. It stated she liked a drink and one of her pastimes was to go to the local rugby club with friends. Consequently, I hadn't really interacted with her as her interests were different to mine. Anne-Marie sent me a private message checking in on me as she sensed something wasn't right. We exchanged several messages (roughly 5 hours' worth) talking in general and about our lives. This messaging continued for three days near enough non-stop. Throughout this time, Anne-Marie kept telling me I should make the trip to visit my stepmum. In the end I told her I'd go if she came with me, I didn't expect her to agree though. So we planned for me to travel to Scarborough on the Saturday morning.

I had already learned so much about Anne-Marie through our openness during our messages, talking about our past lives. Anne-Marie had been out in her Covid bubble the night before I drove up, so there was no need for me to have an early start. I left Norwich around 08:00 with a four-and-a-half-hour drive ahead of me. The sun was shining so I enjoyed a leisurely drive. I stopped at Kings Lynn to pick up some refreshments en route along with a pack of donuts for her children. Once I turned off the A17, I was in unknown territory, but was experiencing some lovely views which only improved the further I travelled. I recall going over the Humber Bridge for the first time, passing Beverley where my dad had worked a couple of years previously, and as I passed Driffield with a sign telling me 22 miles to Scarborough my phone rang. It was Anne-Marie asking if I was getting close. I arrived in Scarborough and parked outside her house, sending a message saying I was here and lit a cigarette. Her door opened and there she stood.

After our initial greeting, Anne-Marie took me inside to meet her children, five of her six were present and after handing over the donuts and introductions we all went for a walk along North Bay so I got to see the beach. I bought us all ice-creams at a stand halfway along North Bay. It was decided we wouldn't visit my stepmum as I had heard from her en route and she told me not to bother and to enjoy my weekend as she was feeling in a much better place. I was invited to stay the night, so I didn't have to do all the travelling in one day, which I accepted. I ended up staying the night after also before driving home the following day as I wasn't working till the Tuesday. We had got on well and the children seemed to like me too. We carried on messaging daily. The following weekend, Anne-Marie was away on a course near St. Helen's with work and I had Connor at mine. To my great shock, I received a message telling me she had left the course and was en route to me if that was ok (I don't think she realised the distance). I agreed as this was the first time someone else had made an effort to see me. When Anne-Marie arrived I knew what we had between us was something different. We discussed "us", and decided even though there were one hundred and eighty miles plus between us we would try and make it work. Because of Anne-Marie's children, we decided I would travel twice to her once, but due to Anne-Marie's work, as I was self-employed and not feeling great when I was home alone, I ended up doing more travelling and spending more time in Scarborough than Norwich, making sure I was in Norwich for when I had Connor.

In September, while I was helping to sort out some bits for Anne-Marie I managed to get snapped on a speed camera in Scarborough while doing a tip run with rubbish from her basement. It is what it is. But what made it worse was when travelling back to Norwich eleven hours later in the early hours of the morning I also managed to get caught on an average speed camera.

We booked a joint family holiday at Centre Parcs Sherwood for the end of November, but the 3rd lockdown and its tiers meant we had to change the location to Whinfell. As a combined family we had an amazing break away, spending quality time together and making memories. Straight from Whinfell, we drove to Norwich to take Connor home, but also to visit my nannie as things weren't good. Sadly, she passed away a couple of days later. RIP Nannie.

It wasn't long after this that doing all this travelling unfortunately got the better of me again, and I was flashed on the A17 travelling on a stretch I rarely used as I was following a diversion.

Early the following month, my decree absolute came through, so it was time for me to start making some decisions. I made a few enquiries about my mortgage and found I couldn't have it in my sole name due to my self-employed earnings. So I had to take the tough decision to sell. It was around this time that I started picking up jobs in Scarborough to do while I was there. I arranged to sell through a local Hellesdon agent and my house sale was due to go live on Boxing Day. Three days later I had a viewing that coincided with me taking Connor home. An hour after the viewing I received an offer for my asking price while I was driving down the A17, which I accepted. The sale was quicker than we expected, Anne-Marie suggested I move to Scarborough. It didn't take much thought. We agreed a plan for me to start moving bits on my trips back and forth to Norwich.

In the March, I decided to sell my car as having nine points on my license would put my insurance through the roof, and with no off-road parking it was the best option all round as I still had my trusty van for work purposes. In the same month, I decided to pay Angie off with my inheritance from nannie. It was such a relief to get Angie out of my life finally. I was free to start my fresh life in Scarborough and was added to the tenancy agreement on 1st April.

I kept in touch with very few people from my life in Norwich, but when I saw that Chris and his family were moving back to the States I had to stop at Mildenhall and say my farewells as they did more for me than they realise in the time I knew them. They are forever friends and we still keep tabs on each other through Facebook.

It was around this time I contacted a local security firm who supplied staff for Scarborough Open Air Theatre so I could work there when they had performances.

My house sale eventually completed in the July, taking longer than expected due to issues in the buyers' chain, so depending how you look at it, you could say this is when I officially moved to Scarborough. This is also the time I changed my access arrangements for Connor to just alternate weekends. To this day, I still drive to Norwich and back every other Friday, returning on the Sunday to take him home.

Now everything from my old life was dealt with, and with Anne-Marie and I getting on so well I started planning my engagement surprise. I'd done a fair bit of work for The Green Rooms, refurbished upstairs into another restaurant area instead of a hair salon, and as this was our favourite restaurant I decided it was an easy choice, especially since the owners were family friends of Anne-Marie and her family.

I made excuses prior to the day, saying they needed to see me about further works while I was doing my planning with them. I told Anne-Marie that we had a last-minute table booked on the day in case something else had messed my plan up and that we had to dress smart as we were having a business meeting with the owners while we were there. The restaurant was full, we were sat in a corner and I could tell the staff all knew by the looks I was getting. I was nervous enough without the stares. Just after we finished eating our main course I was expecting the owner to come and ask if I would pop and see the chef quickly. Instead she rushed down the stairs and over to our table in a panic, asking me to go upstairs as a customer was holding a shelf which had come unattached. Obviously in panic I rushed upstairs to be handed a platter they had made with the ring placed on top that I'd dropped in earlier. Downstairs, other customers were asking Anne-Marie if everything was okay. She was in two minds as to whether to rush home and get my drill, knowing I had no tools with me. A waitress who knew us both noticed this and went over to start a conversation, knowing what was happening. With adrenaline pumping I made my way down the stairs, slipping and nearly dropping the platter. I walked over to the table and dropped to one knee. I was struggling to get the words out but was fortunate: the Chef had written "Will you marry me" on the platter in chocolate drizzle. Happily, Anne-Marie said YES.

As a family we travelled to Holland-on-Sea for my nanny's 100th birthday and witnessed her opening her birthday card from the Queen.

We weren't rushing to get married as Anne-Marie wanted to go halves on everything. We had planned a date over two years in the future and had most things planned and booked before we went away for another joint family holiday to Centre Parcs Sherwood in the November.

I had heard about a charity called ANDYSMANCLUB and had planned to go along for a while, but due to other family commitments I didn't go until the May. I wasn't wanting to attend for myself, but after attending for a few weeks I could tell how beneficial it was for myself as well, and in the August I was asked to become a facilitator. Being a facilitator involves guiding the conversation within group, supply support for other users with empathy and hopefully with previous knowledge or experience.

After attending ANDYSMANCLUB for a couple of weeks I realised there was more to mental health than I realised, so I searched online for a short course to give me more of an insight. While doing the course, after submitting a section for marking, feedback received suggested I role play scenarios instead of using my own personal experiences. Carrying out this course made me realise how many symptoms of various mental health issues I deal with daily. Personally, I have only visited a medical professional for help or guidance on one occasion regarding these so I have no official diagnosis. In truth, I don't wish for one either. I gained my TQUK Level

2 Certificate in Awareness of Mental Health Problems in the August.

On our first holiday abroad, we went to Benidorm (Connor's first ever holiday abroad) in the September. I'd paid for 7 of us to have an all-inclusive holiday but due to complications two of the older children couldn't go. The day before we flew, I drove to Norwich to collect Connor, drove home and got a couple of hours rest before driving everyone to Manchester airport for the flight. It was a much-needed break for us all. On our return to the UK we had to drive straight to Norwich to ensure that Connor was back in time for school. En route we had an issue that nearly broke us up as a family but fortunately we resolved the issue. A lot of this was down to us all being overtired.

Life as a family always has its difficulties, especially with teenagers involved. Several occasions have tested Anne-Marie's and my relationship. The worst must have been in the December when Anne-Marie asked me to help with discipline, and her youngest daughter didn't agree with me and punched me in the face. Anne-Marie told me to report it to the police due to other factors that had gone on with the family.

In the July, my nanny in Holland-on-Sea went to heaven and Anne-Marie and I travelled down for her funeral and final resting place alongside my granddad. RIP Nanny.

This same month I also joined IAM (Institute of Advanced Motorists) and passed with a F1RST, according to the F1RST register I am the first Dunkin to achieve this pass grade.

Around this time, I quoted some work for a local church and when I completed the works something was telling me to invoice 50% less, so I did. Three or four weeks later, when working a security shift at Scarborough Open Air Theatre I received a call informing me I had won £9500 worth of 40v Makita tools (Him upstairs looks after me) from an online competition I had entered.

In September I went to Nottingham on my stag do, organised kindly by my best man Phil. It was a fun-packed weekend which involved being dressed up as a woman, doing all manner of activities including whitewater rafting, a parkrun, escape room, bowling, a drag show and karting to name a few. Incidentally, I managed to get myself banned from the karting due to an incident in the last race where I lost my cool over another driver breaking the rules. Strangely, no video footage of the last race was ever forwarded to us.

My wedding day to Anne-Marie will always hold many happy memories. I ensured no one from my previous relationships were included, except family who attended. The day started with Phil and me doing a drive by with music blaring past the hotel where Anne-Marie stayed the night. Phil and I had a coffee in town thirty minutes before we were due at the hotel, I organised Dunkin Donuts for the guests to have after the service. My speech had no preparation, so it came unprompted from my heart. The evening went as planned and was enjoyed by all the guests we'd invited to celebrate this special occasion with us.

EPILOGUE

Well that's my life. I am who I am because of all the good and bad things that have happened to me and I am proud of the person I have become. I have two biological children, six stepchildren and seven grandchildren who all inspire me and keep me on my toes. Many people wish things didn't happen to them or wish they had done things differently. Not me though, because if the things in my life had not happened to me I wouldn't be the person I am today with the positive, happy-go-lucky attitude I have and knowing that there is always tomorrow which will hold happiness if I let it. I frequently use phrases like: Hakuna Matata; sh!t happens; it is what it is; no pain no gain; I'm all right, it's them others; what doesn't kill you makes you stronger.

I do have my beliefs and I am a Christian; it has been mentioned in this book as it has played a valuable part of my life. One verse that has always given me strength and comfort is John 3:16-17 'For God so loved the world he gave his one and only Son, that whoever believes in him shall not perish but have eternal life. For God did not send his Son into the world to condemn the world, but to save the world through him'.

Through many stages of my life, I lived with a smile on

my face to hide the pain and disguise what I was dealing with personally. I would assist others with their issues as dealing with their issues would make me forget mine or make them feel less significant.

A few people over the years have said that my life would make a good book and they haven't known half of what has been included in my journey. So hopefully you have enjoyed reading it and understand that it has been written to encourage others to look past the negatives that are happening all around us and concentrate on what happiness the future holds.

I am not someone who worries what others think of me as I know what and who I am. Even though I am someone who needs reassurance in what I do, I put others before myself even though this is less frequent these days. It has been extremely difficult to draft this book and think of the many positives I've included: on my first attempt there were very few.

Since writing this autobiography, even though I believed I had accepted and dealt with things that happened in my life, I am now having regular normal dreams again instead of negative ones which were becoming all too common. I would also like to add that when I read this book as a whole, it affected my mental health for a couple of days, but I soon bounced back to my normal self.

If it had not been for me attending ANDYSMANCLUB a couple of years back (my first introduction was "I'm Mark and I'm a closed book"), I don't think I would ever have had the strength and encouragement to write about my life, so with this in mind I urge any man who is struggling to search online and find your local group.

ANDYSMANCLUB is a free peer-to-peer support group that supplies a place for men (18+) to come together in a safe and open environment to talk about the issues or problems that they have faced or are currently facing. The clubs meet from 7pm to 9pm every Monday (excluding bank holidays) but men are urged to get there earlier for a free brew and biscuits .

Obviously, I have mentioned a couple of male mental health groups in this book, but I know there are groups out there for women also, one I know of is WOMENS WELL-BEING CLUB groups, which meet nationwide every Tuesday if you need a safe place to talk.

FOOTPRINTS

One night, a man had a dream.
He dreamed he was walking along
the beach with the Lord.
Across the sky flashed scenes from his life.
For each scene,
he noticed two sets of footprints in the sand;
one belonged to him,
and the other to the Lord.
When the last scene of his life flashed before him,
he looked back at the footprints in the sand.
He noticed that at many times
across the path of his life,
there was only one set of footprints.
He also noticed that it happened at the very lowest
and sad times of his life,
This really bothered him and
He questioned the Lord about it.
"Lord, you said that once I followed you,
you'd walk with me all the way. But I have noticed
that during the most troublesome times of my life,
there is only one set of footprints

I don't understand why,
when I needed you the most, you would leave me".
The Lord replied, "My precious, precious child
I love you and I would never leave you.
During your times of trial
and suffering when you only saw one set of
footprints,
it was then that I carried you".

Author unknown

ACKNOWLEDGEMENTS

This book has been written to give thanks to everyone
who has played a part in my life.

With special appreciation to anyone who is named and
whose role in my life has made an impact.

Also a special mention to Anne-Marie for prompting me
to put pen to paper and Kevin Ward who kindly assisted me
with my editing, grama and punctuation.

The two poems included in this publication:
Don't Give Up and Footprints, were given to me in my
teenage years and have always been remembered in difficult
times.

9 781805 178606